# THE NONPROFIT COMMUNICATIONS ENGINE

A leader's guide to
managing mission-driven
marketing and communications

Published by
Big Duck Studio, Inc.
Brooklyn, NY 11201

For bulk orders contact hello@bigduck.com

Printed in the United States of America
First edition, 2019

Library of Congress Control Number: 2019911701

ISBN: 978-1-7333553-0-8

1 2 3 4 5 6 7 8 9

# THE NONPROFIT COMMUNICATIONS ENGINE

### A leader's guide to managing mission-driven marketing and communications

## BY SARAH DURHAM

For all the Ducks.

# CONTENTS

# INTRODUCTION

**"The world is before you
and you need not take it
or leave it as it was
when you came in."**

~ James Baldwin

Gemma joined the staff of a nonprofit with a mission that inspired her after many years working for companies she didn't truly believe in. She started in a mid-level programs position and worked her way up to become the program's manager and then director. After a few years, she moved into a new C-suite role where she had oversight for all of the organization's programs, reported to the executive director, and regularly presented at board meetings. Gemma was at the core of the organization's mission and trusted by its leadership, so it wasn't surprising when she was offered the job after the executive director left.

Although she knew the organization well, Gemma spent the first few months as CEO deepening her understanding of areas within the organization where her experience was limited.

The development director gave Gemma a dashboard of the fundraising metrics her team used, shared details of the team's strengths and opportunities, and gave her books to read on fundraising best practices. She invited her to department meetings, brought her to lunch with donors, and recommended a few industry conferences where Gemma could learn more about fundraising.

The operations director and finance team gave Gemma a similar overview. She reviewed budget-versus-actual reports, past audits, and HR dashboards. Once again, Gemma was given a stack of reference books and a list of trade associations she could join or conferences she might attend to learn best practices.

But when Gemma sat down with the communications director, the conversation was different. There were no dashboards and few metrics. Instead, she reviewed recently produced materials and an editorial calendar.

The communications director talked about the challenges of getting the newsletter out on time, sourcing articles and other content from the staff, and budgeting to expand their digital advertising and search engine marketing program. He used terms like *SEO, SEM, conversions, form completions, segmenting, impressions, likes,* and *shares*—terms Gemma was only marginally familiar with.

Gemma wasn't at all certain how the details fit together and supported the organization's larger goals. Who were they trying to reach? What were they hoping all of this would achieve? Were the communications they produced intended to reach and engage donors, clients, activists, or policymakers? Were they issue- or program-specific or more general? How did the people they needed to reach and work with perceive the organization?

To manage communications in this nonprofit effectively, Gemma realized she needed a clearer overview that would help her assess what was working and what was not without getting lost in all the details. But how to do that, especially with all the other things competing for Gemma's time and attention?

Like Gemma, most executive directors emerge from fundraising or programs—not from a communications background. They have worked on fundraising campaigns that raise money, advocacy campaigns that change hearts and minds around a particular issue, and recruiting clients for programs. But most executive directors lack experience weaving together all these areas so their nonprofit's communications feel cohesive and represent their organization's voice effectively, without fragmentation or disconnects. Other leaders simply don't prioritize communications.

But what would it be like if they did? What would it be like if more CEOs set a goal of "blowing the roof off their communications," as Vince Warren, CEO of the Center for Constitutional Rights, opted to do in 2018? Would these nonprofits no longer be hidden gems? Would their reputations precede them? Would they more swiftly and effectively change hearts and minds and achieve results?

This book is intended to help executive directors, CEOs, board members, and other nonprofit leaders optimize nonprofit communications by providing them with a simple framework that transcends specific tools and tactics. It offers a bigger-picture perspective that can be applied to organizations of varied sizes, ages, and levels of capacity—not just those that are older or more established.

The following pages won't cover how many emails a nonprofit should send, how to craft an eye-catching newsletter, how to get the most out of a PR team, or other tasks of day-to-day communications management. Those will all change, particularly as new technologies emerge. Instead, we will focus on what comes *before* all the tactics—overarching communications goals—and the capacity a nonprofit needs in order to achieve and maintain those goals regardless of how big, small, new, or well-established it is.

The first chapter, *Getting clearer about communications*, includes a high-level summary of this framework, an outline of the barriers that most nonprofits face, and a tool to assess your organization's communications capacity. It will help you clarify what success looks like for your organization's communications and identify some of the obstacles. The chapters that follow unpack each of the six core components essential to building a strong communications engine.

# CHAPTER 1:
# GETTING CLEARER ABOUT EFFECTIVE COMMUNICATIONS

## DEFINING SUCCESSFUL COMMUNICATIONS

Whether your organization is working to cure cancer, shelter or feed people, create safer streets, advocate for equality, or create change in another way, you've got a mission. A nonprofit's mission is the fundamental reason it exists and defines the work it will do to create positive change. Nonprofit missions move the needle on issues, change behaviors, change minds, and inspire action.

In healthy nonprofits, the mission is visible, alive, and flourishing. Even when people can't recite the mission statement verbatim, they understand the essence of the work, who it will help, and why it's beneficial.

Most nonprofit departments have clear mandates and fit together like puzzle pieces. Programs staff bring the mission of a nonprofit to life through programs and services. Development advances the mission by raising money. Operations supports the rest of the organization's work with infrastructure. Each has a specific audience (or audiences) that they must reach and engage.

But if you ask 10 different people to articulate the purpose of their communications or marketing team, you will get 10 different answers. Most of those answers will be murky or focused solely on tactics and channels ("They're the people who keep our website up to date" or "They're the folks who make our brochures"). That's because communications teams have varied and unique responsibilities in different organizations. Communications is more like the shellac on the puzzle or its cardboard backing: intrinsic to the overall stability, reliability, and appearance of the whole organization, but not a neatly defined, separate puzzle piece on its own.

At the National Latina Institute for Reproductive Health (*www.latinainstitute.org*), communications largely supports advocacy and movement-building goals. Its small communications team works with bilingual media and community activists to elevate voices and advance the solutions that best serve their communities.

At the Healthy Materials Lab (*www.healthymaterialslab.org*), communications is focused on educating architects and interior designers about the impact of toxic building materials. The comms team works in service of advancing core programs.

At the Multiple Myeloma Research Foundation (*www.themmrf.org*), communications supports fundraising by creating useful tools to engage donors with their mission and groundbreaking science.

All these communications teams are working to advance the mission of their organization and shape how their issues are perceived, using whatever resources are available given their nonprofit's unique size, structure, and needs—and they all do it a bit differently.

*What would it be like if your organization did a phenomenal job of communicating? Would your nonprofit be a household name with a deep base of regular supporters who donate, volunteer, and take other actions easily? Or would you be a force for good that inspires loyal support from a deeply engaged but selective base?*

While many executive directors struggle to articulate what "great communications" means for their organization, they recognize its absence or failure. Communications is an engine that helps power other essential functions of the organization: If it's not working well, then programs, development, advocacy, and other mission-critical functions are likely to suffer.

Our sector needs a clearer, more widely shared definition for how communications supports nonprofit missions. This definition should reflect how varied and interconnected with other departments communications can be.

> Nonprofit communications is the practice of creating and sustaining mindshare and engagement that advances the mission.

A practice requires repeated effort; it's something we must do over and over again. In practices like meditation, exercise, playing an instrument, yoga, and others, the work is never actually complete. Stop exercising and you lose the benefits of exercise. Stop eating or sleeping well and you feel lousy. Nonprofits must constantly practice communicating effectively, both internally and externally, or they increase the risk that a lack of connection will make it hard to reach, engage, and collaborate with the audiences who are essential to advancing their mission. The practice of establishing connections—or, more specifically, mindshare and engagement—is ongoing, no matter how old, large, or successful a nonprofit becomes.

Mindshare and engagement (which we'll explore more deeply in the following chapter) are strategies to build connections and relationships with an organization, issue, or movement. Fundraisers and senior leadership likely have relationships with major donors. Programs staff have relationships with key partners and peer organizations. All of them rely on effective communications to keep the people they have relationships with engaged.

When a nonprofit communicates successfully, external audiences (individuals, other organizations, foundations, etc.) become aware of and engaged with its mission. They take action to advance the organization or the issues it serves—hopefully more than once. Staff and board recruitment also benefit from effective external communications because candidates with experience in the field may be more likely to know of the organization. Relationships between staff and the people they work with grow deeper and stronger through the organization's marketing and communications efforts. In short, an effective communications engine powers the mission.

## What would great communications achieve?

A decade or so ago, my business was at a critical inflection point. I was managing a series of personal and professional changes, navigating a recession, and making many decisions with long-term implications. The day before I left for a much-needed vacation on Cape Cod, a mentor tasked me with an exercise to help me get some perspective. *Take a walk alone on the beach*, they suggested, *with the sole purpose of imagining the future. Don't bring paper, pens, or spreadsheets—just your imagination. Step into the future and have a good look around. What will it be like? What will you be doing? Who will be there with you?*

Days later, I found myself alone on Cahoon Hollow Beach, walking north. I imagined the clients my company would be working with and the impact our work would have on them. I imagined my staff capable not only of doing this great work but of collaborating with each other in new ways. I returned from my walk feeling affirmed that the business was essentially on track, and clearer about a few areas that I needed to focus on.

Since then, I've encouraged many nonprofit CEOs and other leaders to try this exercise, too (no beach required).

*Imagine your nonprofit in the not-too-distant-future enjoying a moment of great success. What would that be like? How would things have changed? Who would be on the team?*

What would your organization's desired future look like? You might begin to answer that question by describing your programs—perhaps the number of clients you'd be serving, the positive changes in their lives, or the state of key issues you advocate for.

Now imagine how a truly effective communications function could support those outcomes. What would that enable? Would people who currently don't know you exist become aware of your work and inspired to get involved? Would organizations you want to partner with be more eager to collaborate with you? Would your staff be able to write or speak more accurately, effectively, and consistently about what you do? Would you no longer be a best-kept secret?

Before you read on, jot down your own vision of success for your organization's communications. As you reflect on the ideas in this book, perhaps this vision will evolve into a mandate or North Star you can use to make decisions, affirm what's working, and prioritize changes in your organization's communications.

# BARRIERS TO SUCCESSFUL COMMUNICATIONS

Now that you've considered what success might look like for your organization's communications function, let's get clear about what may be standing in the way of making that a reality. In addition to the lack of a clear mandate, a number of other variables conspire to make building and maintaining an effective nonprofit communications function a challenge.

## Scarcity of skilled professionals

Many nonprofit organizations struggle to find experienced professionals with all three types of expertise that are helpful today: *nonprofit, communications strategy,* and *digital.*

Nonprofit communications used to be largely driven by media relations. Communications staff wrote press releases, helped journalists develop stories, and got coverage in major news outlets if they were successful. Then the digital revolution created seismic shifts in how we all live and work. The channels and tools we use to communicate as individuals and institutions exploded with new options, many of which are free or affordable for the first time. And they keep changing.

Being a communications professional in *any* industry has required pioneering and innovating in the wilderness over the past two decades. Professional communicators must adapt, create, and hack their way through this fast-changing world with a constantly shifting array of tools, many of which must be adapted for nonprofit-sector agendas. That never-ending state of learning and experimenting can be exhilarating, but it's also time-consuming and distracting. When we're lost in the weeds of figuring out Facebook's newest algorithms or how the latest marketing automation software works, it can be easy to lose sight of the bigger picture.

Organizations try to keep up by hiring and promoting digitally savvy staff into communications roles despite their lack of marketing education or experience. This increases the organization's digital capacity, but it can also create challenges: a tactics-first culture where goals aren't clearly articulated or advanced, for instance, or interpersonal tensions when staff are perceived as junior.

Other nonprofits hire marketing and communications professionals from the for-profit sector, hoping they'll be able to increase the organization's communications capacity. People from the corporate sector are often attracted to the idea of working for social good, but the realities of building buy-in, significantly reduced resources, and the lack of bottom-line clarity common in nonprofit environments can be demotivating and challenging.

## Unicorn communicators

Organizations search for communications staff with an impossible-to-find set of skills and talents. These "unicorn" communicators are expected to facilitate the flow of communications internally and effectively market the entire organization single-handedly. They are asked to write, design, and coordinate every aspect of communications—and even (perhaps) manage a program or two.

The search for this magical creature is often motivated by a healthy desire to reduce the communications work for others and centralize this function. But if the people hired don't meet these high expectations, others may form a negative set of beliefs about them and the work itself may suffer.

## Key people hold the cards

Because they often work solo or with just a few others in their department (especially those unicorn communicators), individual staff responsible for communications build up a lot of institutional memory. They often start, oversee, and execute projects independently without documenting processes, passwords, and other details that ensure someone else can step in and take over if necessary. This lack of documentation and sharing of knowledge reinforces a silo-focused culture and is debilitating when key people leave or are absent. It can also centralize power unproductively, creating barriers to collaboration.

## Inconsistency, noise, and mixed messages

Staff across all departments regularly write, speak, tweet, and post about their work, so everyone in a nonprofit is a communicator these days. Few nonprofits create communications guidelines and messaging to help them describe the work clearly and accurately, so staff end up winging it and can easily go off message without even realizing it.

Message coordination between departments can also fall by the wayside. It's common for different departments to send out emails at the same time or describe the work in very different ways. This clutters up inboxes and sows confusion and annoyance among the external audience. Odds increase that the people who get these messages will just ignore what they see, hear, and read.

## Resources don't match needs

Most founders in the for-profit world wouldn't dream of beginning a start-up without expert marketers in their C-suite. Skilled marketing staff, armed with viable budgets for their department, are the norm in the corporate sector. Nonprofits, on the other hand, rarely add marketing or communications people to their team in the first few years, nor can they typically allocate the resources these departments need to achieve their organization's goals. Culturally, the nonprofit sector isn't used to thinking of marketing or communications as an essential component of building a successful nonprofit from the ground up.

Communications and marketing jobs in nonprofits are often staffed by fundraisers, program managers, or administrators with minimal relevant experience, other primary work responsibilities, and tiny budgets for professional development. CEOs are struggling to keep up, too. Most nonprofit executive directors and CEOs have backgrounds in programs or fundraising, not communications. Executive directors have even less time to keep up with the latest communications and marketing strategies and how they might be applied to their work. They often struggle to staff, budget, manage, set clear goals, or structure communications effectively.

## Organizational silos

When departments function like warring or competing groups, their organization is more likely to communicate externally in disconnected, inconsistent ways because there's little alignment, coordination, or effort to speak with one voice.

## THREE OUTCOMES OF SUCCESSFUL COMMUNICATIONS

Earlier in this chapter, we explored the goals and obstacles of a successful communications discipline. But how do you know if your communications efforts are truly moving the needle? How do you set targets and measure progress?

There are three primary outcomes a successful communications practice can achieve that will help advance the mission. They are:

> **Engagement:** The right people know, remember, and connect with your organization and work, then take meaningful action on its behalf.
>
> **Clear voice:** Your organization's voice is clear, credible, compelling, and consistent at all points of contact.
>
> **Sustainable momentum:** Your organization's communications are not dependent on an individual.

These outcomes can be achieved whether communications is a separate function or embedded within other departments and jobs. They are also important outcomes whether your goal is to communicate on behalf of a program, issue, movement, or organization.

## Engagement

Fostering engagement with your organization is everyone's job, not just the people with "communications" or "marketing" in their job description. Engagement is mission-critical and touches every department's work. The programs and advocacy staff brings the mission to life. The development team advances the mission by raising money to support those programs. Effective communications generates the mindshare and engagement that supports it all.

Managing engagement effectively requires understanding who the organization's target audiences are, what actions they should take to advance the mission, what resources can be dedicated to inspiring those actions, and how to measure the results. This is the most important place to start for organizations building their communications capacity from scratch, and where most communications resources will be allocated. Engagement work requires deep collaboration between communications staff and their peers in other departments.

## Clear voice

Founders are typically effective communicators who are able to write and speak about the organization powerfully and consistently because they are expressing their own vision. But as an organization grows and more people start writing, speaking, and producing materials independently, it becomes more challenging to express a vision clearly and consistently.

An organization whose voice is clear, credible, compelling, and consistent at all points of contact takes its audiences down a more clearly illuminated, direct path toward engagement. Dedicated communications staff typically lead an organization's efforts to unify messaging, visuals, and tone.

## Sustainable momentum

When one person controls all communications, there's an intrinsic risk of failure when they are no longer part of the team. As an organization grows, the "roll up our sleeves and get it all done" culture that is typically led by the founder or a select few people must be replaced with sustainable momentum that can be maintained by a broader group with different talents. This is particularly true in communications because it connects people with the organization—often replenishing donors, clients, and others who've fallen away. Engagement falters without sustainable momentum.

## THE SIX ELEMENTS THAT POWER SUCCESSFUL COMMUNICATIONS OUTCOMES

There are six core components that a nonprofit can leverage to improve its engagement, develop its voice, and create sustainable momentum in its communications.

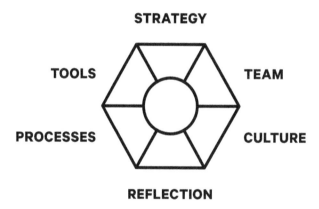

### Strategy

An organization's goals and objectives should inform its communications strategies and tactics, beginning with its strategic plan and department-specific objectives.

### Team

Staff, volunteers, freelancers, consultants, and others power the engine of a nonprofit's communications.

## Culture

Collaboration and organizational norms shape how people treat each other and influence how communications are prioritized.

## Tools

The assets and resources the organization allocates to communications advance or limit effectiveness.

## Processes

Defined methods for how tasks are approached more predictably yield a desired communications result.

## Reflection

Reviewing the effectiveness of their work helps people understand and improve communications outcomes.

These six components power communications regardless of an organization's size, age, or mission. If one of them is weak, inadequate, or challenged, it is harder for communicators to build engagement, manage the organization's voice, and create sustainable momentum. This, in turn, reduces their capacity to advance the mission. The executive director and other organization leaders control these elements. In fact, the people who are responsible for communications often have limited or no control over many of the elements they need to build and maintain a communications engine. This is one of many key reasons why trust and collaboration between communicators and C-suite leadership is essential to success.

# SELF-ASSESSMENT

This self-assessment will help you benchmark your organization's communications capacity and prioritize your efforts to optimize it. Consider asking others on your team to complete this self-assessment, too, and discuss how your results align or deviate.

### SCALE:

| | | |
|---|---|---|
| 2 | = | Very Satisfied |
| 1 | = | Satisfied |
| 0 | = | Unsure |
| -1 | = | Dissatisfied |
| -2 | = | Very Dissatisfied |

## Rating your current outcomes

The right people know, remember, and connect with us, taking meaningful action that helps advance our mission.

*Satisfaction score:*


Our organization's voice is clear, credible, compelling, and consistent at each point of contact.

*Satisfaction score:*


Our organization's communications function has sustainable momentum that's not dependent on an individual.

*Satisfaction score:*


How satisfied are you with the outcomes your organization's current communications function is achieving? *Tally your scores from the three questions above and add any comments here. Maximum achievable score: 6 points.*


Which outcome does your team produce most effectively?

Which outcome(s) could be improved?

## Identifying where your communications effort needs work

### Strategy

Our organization is clear who its target audiences are, has a strategy to reach and engage them, and has solid plans to implement that strategy.

*Satisfaction score:*

### Team

We have the right people directing, managing, and implementing our organization's communications. The structure of their role works well for the organization.

*Satisfaction score:*

### Culture

Our organization's expectations for staff collaboration and behavior encourage healthy internal and external communications.

*Satisfaction score:*

**Tools**

We have the people, brand elements, content, media, campaigns, software, and other resources our organization needs to communicate effectively.

*Satisfaction score:*

**Processes**

Our communications team has useful written workflows to achieve outcomes predictably without relying on memory.

*Satisfaction score:*

**Reflection**

Our organization consistently gathers data and uses insights to get smarter and to communicate more effectively.

*Satisfaction score:*

**RESULTS**

*Maximum achievable score: 12 points.*

Which of these six areas are you most satisfied with?

Which of these six areas are you least satisfied with?

You have just visualized what successful communications would mean within your organization and considered what's working and what's not using this self-assessment. Now it's time to explore the six core components that will help you bring that vision to life.

It is worth repeating this self-assessment annually to review how your organization's communications evolve over time.

Before you read on, consider starting a document or a notebook you can use to capture your own ideas. Begin by refining your vision for successful communications at your nonprofit. What is the desired state you hope to achieve? Summarize how you feel about your current communications outcomes and capacity. What's working and what's not? As you read and reflect on the six core components in the chapters that follow, capture notes that will help you optimize your organization's communications.

# CHAPTER 2

## STRATEGY

"We need to stop interrupting
what people are interested in
and *be* what people are interested in."

~ Craig Davis, former Chief Creative Officer at J. Walter Thompson

## WHY STRATEGY MATTERS

**Strategy** is the practice of defining what you want to achieve and identifying the best ways to achieve it.

A useful communications strategy begins with a clear understanding of who you are trying to reach (your organization's primary audiences) and the resources you have at your disposal to reach and engage them. It outlines:

> **Goals:** the big-picture statements of what you are striving to achieve
>
> **Objectives:** the measurable outcomes that indicate you've achieved your goals
>
> **Strategies:** the specific approaches that guide your actions and decisions in the service of your goals
>
> **Tactics:** the action steps you take to carry out your strategies

Goals, objectives, strategies, and tactics shift depending on your vantage point and aren't always developed in a linear fashion. For instance, an organization may set a goal to become the leading nonprofit supporting people with disabilities in its community. Its objectives may be to grow recognition for its work and increase donations from new sources. While everyone in the organization ultimately works to support this goal, each department may have its own goals and objectives that emerge from this, or unique strategies that reflect their functional area. Communications may set a strategy to conduct frequent public events throughout the city and measure success by attendance and participation. Development may focus on a digital acquisition strategy and set an objective of getting new people to take action online. Programs will focus on best-of-class service delivery.

In 2012, Transportation Alternatives (*www.transalt.org*), an organization making New York City's streets safer for bicycling, walking, and other modes of transportation, began a strategic planning process. It had grown substantially since its founding in 1973 and become well-known for an ambitious vision.

The best strategic planning processes create time and space for conversations that dig into the heart of an organization, challenging assumptions and affirming truths. Transportation Alternatives' staff and board dove into the process headfirst, exploring key issues at the core of their work. How could they reduce car-related crashes citywide? How could they serve all New Yorkers—not just those living in the most affluent or politically influential neighborhoods?

Through strategic planning, Transportation Alternatives' leadership affirmed the organization's mission "to reclaim New York City's streets from the automobile and advocate for better bicycling, walking, and public transit for all New Yorkers." But what was the smartest strategy to achieve that goal?

After exploring options and pressure-testing a few ideas, the planning group settled on a powerful strategy: to focus on New York City's arterial streets. These large public thoroughfares represent only 15% of the city's streets, yet most traffic-related fatalities occur on them. By focusing their efforts on changing arterial streets—not *all* streets—the team set in motion a way to make decisions, prioritize their work, and impact New Yorkers in all five boroughs.

Transportation Alternatives set clear, measurable objectives to create "complete streets" (designed for safe biking, walking, driving, and public transportation) and got to work. The organization's progress has been impressive. By 2018, it had achieved redesigns on some of New York City's most notorious arterial streets including Grand Concourse in the Bronx, Amsterdam Avenue on Manhattan's Upper West Side, and Queens Boulevard, which has long been known as the "Boulevard of Death." This focus on arterial streets coincided with a year-over-year decrease in traffic deaths for five years straight (from 299 in 2013 to an all-time low of 202 in 2018).

Some strategic plans articulate goals and strategies that more obviously require communications expertise and leadership to achieve, such as *expand our network, increase our visibility, or get our internal stakeholders aligned.* Other organizational goals like those articulated in Transportation Alternatives' strategic plan require communications to play a more backstage or supportive role by working collaboratively with peers in other departments.

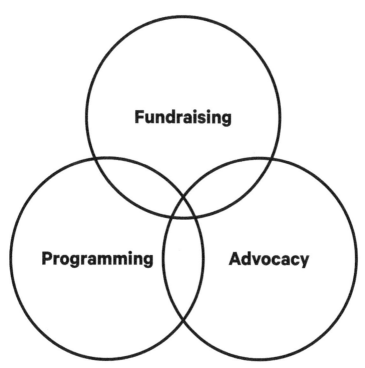

*Many communications goals and objectives are developed to support those of an organization's fundraising, programs, and advocacy efforts.*

A strategic plan that calls for reaching and engaging a new type of donor, for example, can be supported by developing a donor communications content program and calendar, ensuring that all prospect data is correctly set up in a database, and developing personalized ways to engage them. An organizational goal to reach and engage new activists or volunteers might be supported with robust digital content that attracts people who are passionate about the issue, giving them reasons to provide their email address and engaging them online so they are motivated to take action.

Corporate Accountability (*www.corporateaccountability.org*) wages "strategic campaigns that compel transnational corporations, and the governments that do their bidding to stop destroying our health, human rights, democracy, and planet." To achieve this mission, it uses a strategy of organizing people to apply pressure on corporations, which requires deep collaboration between communications and programs staff. Generating media visibility is a key tactic they use to bring this strategy to life.

When strategic planning causes a significant shift in the organization's work, communications will likely change, too. Asking these questions after strategic planning can identify if you need to rethink your communications function:

- Does our strategic plan suggest that we need to establish new communications goals or objectives?

- Which of our current communications strategies, tactics, and channels should change based on what we're trying to achieve as an organization?

- Does our strategic plan require reaching or engaging different or new audiences?

- Does our current brand strategy or brand identity need to change to align with our new strategic direction?

- Will the resources allocated to communications be adequate to advance this plan?

Tactics bring a strategy to life and consume the majority of time spent by nonprofit communicators. They should emerge from communications goals and objectives established by larger organizational or departmental goals and objectives. Good communications strategy also depends on clarity about the audiences that must be engaged to achieve those goals.

# UNDERSTANDING THE AUDIENCES YOU'RE REACHING

As consumers, we frequently conduct transactions with businesses whose products and services we use, so they become household names. From the coffee we drink to the sneakers we wear, many big brands stick in our minds because we interact with dozens of them every day.

But our relationship with nonprofit brands are different: less transactional and far less frequent when compared with the coffee we consume, computers we use, or clothes we wear. A 2016 survey by the Bureau of Labor Statistics[1] showed that only 25% of Americans volunteer their time, for example. Many donate regularly, or become members of an arts organization or community center, but even they don't engage on a daily basis. Still others participate in programs, sign pledges, show up at marches, and participate in legislative fly-ins—sporadically or occasionally. As potential clients, donors, or voters, we all receive emails and mailings and view ads from nonprofit organizations, too. Many organizations want us to take action on their behalf—more regularly than we probably will. Mission-driven organizations strive to reach:

- **Donors and supporters:** individuals, corporations, and foundations that support an organization's work financially

---

1     *www.bls.gov/news.release/pdf/volun.pdf*

- **Programs audiences:** prospective and existing clients, members, peer organizations, and partners

- **Advocates:** activists, policymakers, and institutions that take action on issues

- **The media:** journalists, media companies, and influencers who cover topics related to their work or change the conversation

- **Partner and peer organizations:** organizations and influencers they work with and/or who help connect them with clients

- **Internal stakeholders:** board members, staff, volunteers, and others who keep the organization running

Communicating effectively on behalf of an organization requires identifying and engaging the *right* people—those who have good reasons to care about your mission. Once you're clear who they are, prioritizing them forces you to think big-picture and apply strategy. It's the essential first step toward communicating effectively.

The mission of the National Brain Tumor Society (*www.braintumor.org*) is to invest in, mobilize, and unite the brain tumor community to discover a cure, deliver effective treatments, and advocate for patients and care partners. The organization's values clearly state that the patient and care partner community comes first, followed by the professionals (researchers, policymakers, pharma, etc.) who can help them. If we drew its audiences in broad terms, it might look something like this:

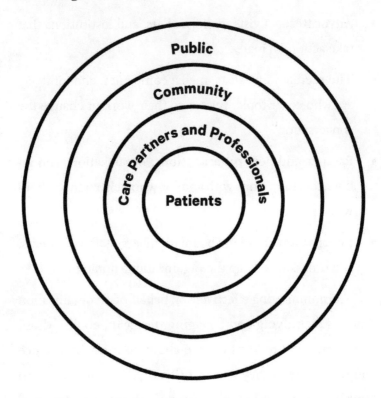

Its leaders would love the National Brain Tumor Society to be a household name, reaching people who aren't affected by brain tumors so they can support the work or find services when someone they know is diagnosed. If they could afford to, they'd mail to every household in America, advertise extensively on digital, print, and TV channels, and more. But it's unlikely they will ever have the resources necessary to reach and engage these outer-ring audiences regularly enough to become a memorable blip on their radar.

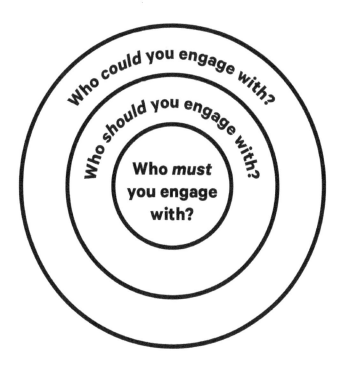

Good strategy begins by identifying the people that you must connect with to bring your strategic plan to life. Consider drawing bull's-eyes like the one above. At the center of each are the people your organization *must* connect and engage with. The next ring are the people your organization *should* connect and engage with. The final layer are the people you *might* connect and engage with.

The outer rings are *useful* to connect with, while the inner rings are *essential* to advance your organization's mission.

Should you spend your limited advertising budget on social media or subway ads? Would blogging help you reach your goals? Or would it be more effective to focus on getting media coverage with the local newspaper and radio stations?

Defining target audiences first is essential to an effective communications strategy because it helps you make important decisions well.

(If you're keeping a notebook with ideas as you read this book, take a moment to jot down your thoughts about the audiences that are most essential for your organization to reach and engage in order to achieve its goals.)

## Personas and mindsets

Communicators often define their audiences in more detailed, human terms using personas and mindsets.

**Personas** are fictionalized stories about the main types of people who interact with your organization. They are stand-ins for different segments of your list that help you turn a category like "donors" into characters you can imagine in more concrete terms.

**Mindsets** are the beliefs that guide people to make decisions and take action. Audience personas and mindsets help everyone in the organization write, design, and speak with particular people in mind by making abstract groups ("donors," "clients," etc.) more real and dimensional.

| Name | Grassroots donor Ginny | |
|---|---|---|
| Demographics | 55-year-old female living in New Jersey. Yearly income is <$99K | |
| Connection to Fountain House | Has a cousin with schizophrenia. Heard about Fountain House through a direct mail piece. Made one gift at year-end. | |
| What she's looking for | She's looking for small ways to get involved with Fountain House and give back beyond donating. | |
| What Fountain House wants | Fountain House wants her to get more involved and eventually make a second gift. | |

*This simple donor persona for Fountain House (www.fountain-house.org), a mental health organization, transforms an abstract category like "donor" into a human staff can understand and connect with, which helps them write and design more persuasive, compelling messages.*

The New York School of Interior Design (*www.nysid.edu*) offers undergraduate, graduate, and continuing education classes to a wide range of students, many of them adults. Despite winning awards for its excellent programs, it experienced inconsistencies in the application and enrollment pipeline. Why did some students apply, get accepted, and then choose not to enroll? Why did some programs fill up quickly while others were harder to fill year after year? What could the school do to market its programs more effectively to the people who'd be most likely to attend if accepted? To answer these questions, the school's leaders dug into their data, analyzing information they had gathered from applicants and students for years.

Staff and consultants examined how much money was spent across all marketing efforts to reach new prospects (historically, through advertising in magazines), factoring in student acceptance and enrollment rates. This research revealed that a significant percentage of accepted students declined to enroll, which generated a loss for the school.

Interviews to understand the mindsets of prospective NYSID students explored why some students accepted and others declined admission. From this research, four primary mindsets of their typical student emerged:

- **Career finders and changers:** primarily people in their 20s and 30s who are considering pursuing a career in interior design; most already have jobs but aren't really committed to what they are currently doing

- **Traditional-aged students:** students who are traditionally college-aged (around 18–23) and do not yet have a bachelor's degree

- **Established professionals:** people who are already practicing interior designers, seeking credentials and greater legitimacy

- **Explorers:** students who are curious about interior design and taking a class or two to fulfill their interests through the Institute for Continuing and Professional Studies

Mapping the school's revenue and admissions data to these segments revealed useful patterns: NYSID's greatest potential for growth lay with career finders and changers.

Past marketing campaigns highlighted the school's robust interior design programs in general terms. Armed with clearer insights on their prospective students' mindsets, the

communications team at NYSID developed campaigns that
spoke more directly to the priorities of their prospective students: finding a career they will love.

The team also defined audience personas—examples of
typical people who fit into each mindset—to make them more
real. This work provided a lens through which everyone at
NYSID could reconsider and realign how they communicate.
Years later, these mindsets continue to drive NYSID's external
communications. Enrollment is up and marketing costs are
down because marketers develop campaigns with a greater
ability to reach and engage the right people.

*Bat Conservation International (www.batcon.org), with help from
a consultant, used social analysis research to identify five "tribes"
that generally engage with its work. Each tribe's attributes were
defined along with the content, communication, and engagement
implications for each group.*

A person's ability to write, design, and communicate will improve significantly when they do so with real people in mind—not abstract categories. This is a skill many CEOs and executive directors who are natural communicators often develop intuitively, but most others in an organization will need guidance, especially if they are creating materials for people they may not know or interact with personally. Communicators can conduct quantitative research (such as surveys or data analysis) and qualitative research (such as interviews or informal focus groups) to identify core audiences, codifying what they uncover into personas that make the abstract real.

## Segmenting

**Segmenting** is dividing audiences into subgroups and communicating with them in even more personalized ways. Designing, creating, and managing segmented campaigns can be much more effective than one-size-fits-all, but creates a lot more work and complexity for communicators. It's most likely to succeed when the communications team has the resources and expertise to manage segmentation well.

There are many ways to segment your audiences, including:

- By issue, interest, or focus (e.g., cat person versus dog person in an animal rights group)

- By demographics (e.g., parents of young children versus adults with no children at home in a community-based organization)

- By mindset (e.g., the beliefs that guide people's perspectives)

- By engagement (e.g., highly versus minimally engaged)

- More than one of the above

NTEN (*www.nten.org*) regularly segments and personalizes its communications in order to help members, who work in nonprofit organizations, engage with the programs that will benefit them the most.

To promote an upcoming advanced course on community engagement strategies, for example, communications staff will query the database to identify people with the words "community" or "outreach" in their job title. If that list is too small, they might also add "communications" job titles to the list or add a segment of people who've taken other fundraising or communications courses over the past year. To hone the list further, they exclude anyone who is already registered for the course and apply a geographic location range. "If we have a Nonprofit Tech Club event coming up in Columbia, MO, that's not very relevant to our subscriber in Juneau, AK. So we decide to send that event email to everyone within a 50-mile radius of Columbia," says Erin Dougherty, a former NTEN digital engagement manager.

Segmenting effectively requires having good data in a constituent relationship management (CRM) system, clarity on the personas and mindsets of your audiences, an understanding of what content will be most relevant to them, and the ability to craft a relevant message that inspires the recipient to take action. What are the segments and what are the personas and mindsets that are most important for your organization to reach and engage?

## BUILDING MINDSHARE AND ENGAGEMENT AMONG TARGET AUDIENCES

Kony 2012. The Girl Effect. First World Problems. The ice bucket challenge. Viral PSAs and other campaigns like these have catapulted organizations and issues from relative obscurity into the spotlight. But for the vast majority of nonprofits, mindshare and engagement are built through long-term focused outreach—not overnight.

Getting the right people to know, connect, and act on behalf of your nonprofit *once* is just the start of a relationship that may or may not help advance the mission. The Fundraising Effectiveness Project (*www.afpfep.org*), an initiative of the Association of Fundraising Professionals that shares fundraising insights gleaned from more than 13,000 nonprofit organizations annually, reports that less than half of all donors give to the same organization two years in a row. Nonprofits work hard to inspire people to act—and even harder to get them to engage repeatedly over time. This is one of the reasons so many organizations today describe themselves as a "best-kept secret" or a "hidden gem." They're doing great work, but never seem to reach people beyond their inner circle. To build an enduring brand, you've got to get on people's radar and stay there. You've got to build **mindshare**.

> **Mindshare** is the level of awareness
> and understanding that a product,
> program, service, or organization
> has in people's minds.

Nonprofits strive to build mindshare so they are top-of-mind when the people who will benefit from their mission or want to support it are ready to take action. What organization will most people donate to when a natural disaster strikes? If they want to help animals in their community? If they are diagnosed with cancer? The organizations you think of first are the ones that have effectively built mindshare with you. Mindshare paves the way for action.

Harris Poll's annual EquiTrend study (*www.theharrispoll. com/equitrend*) polls Americans about their awareness of non-profit brands. The rankings are based on three questions that measure mindshare: how well an individual knows the entity, what they think of it, and whether they want to interact with it. It's that third question—the one about *action*—that is most central to advancing the mission. Actions, even small ones, tell you if you're capturing people's hearts and minds. Actions are also where the individual's motivation and the organization's mission overlap.

Establishing mindshare begins when people become aware of something that is personally relevant or meaningful enough to be worth paying attention to.

The following table illustrates the first steps toward building mindshare.

| Awareness | Relevance | Confirmation | First action |
|---|---|---|---|
| Tanisha is invited to buy a ticket to a gala by her colleague, who serves on the organization's board. | Tanisha likes and respects her colleague. | Tanisha talks with her colleague about the organization and forms a sense of what it does. | Tanisha attends the event. |
| Alex gets an email from an unknown organization asking them to sign a pledge. | Alex is passionate about the issue. | Alex clicks through on the "About Us" link in the email and spends some time poking around the site assessing the credibility of the organization. | Alex signs the pledge. |
| Another parent tells Marcus about a terrific after-school program at a local arts organization. | Marcus wants an enriching after-school option for his child. | Marcus visits the organization's website and asks other parents about it. | Marcus attends an open house to find out more about after-school programs. |
| Seo-yun runs a program at a human services organization. A program participant tells her about a supportive-housing program he benefited from. | Seo-yun has been looking for more supportive-housing partners she can recommend to clients. | Seo-yun calls the supportive-housing program, goes on a tour, and asks a common funder about them. | Seo-yun tells her program director about the program and they agree to start referring clients where appropriate. |

These examples map a journey from zero awareness to first-time engagement. If we expressed this journey as a formula it might be:

**Perceptions + relevance + confirmation = action**

Over time, these experiences feel less relevant as we replace them with newer ideas, memories, and actions. To successfully build mindshare, people must be motivated to stay engaged, and nonprofits must provide them with regular opportunities to do so.

| First Action | Low Motivation/ Lapses | High Motivation/ Engages |
|---|---|---|
| Tanisha attends the event and has a good time. She's moved by the stories she hears. | Tanisha is busy and has her own philanthropic agenda. She ignores subsequent communications from the organization. One year later she remembers the event fondly but doesn't support the organization or remember much about its work. | Tanisha is inspired to get more involved. She reads the materials she receives from the organization after the event, eager to help. One year later she's become a regular donor, made a major gift, and is being courted to join the board. |
| Alex signs a pledge. | Alex is asked to donate after signing the pledge but doesn't feel a connection to the organization yet. They delete the email and forget about it, ignoring subsequent communications. A year later, Alex doesn't recall the pledge or the organization that sent it. | Alex is asked to donate after signing the pledge but doesn't feel a connection to the organization yet. They spend some time researching it online, and feel motivated to support it. They make a gift and start taking other actions. A year later, Alex associates this organization with the issue they are passionate about. |
| Marcus attends an open house to find out more about after-school programs. | Marcus is unimpressed with the program and has other good options for his child's after-school enrichment. A year later, he remembers that he didn't like the program—but not much else about it. | Marcus is impressed with the program and enrolls his child. His connection and regular visits help him get to know the organization. In time, he signs his family up for other programs, attends performances, and donates. A year later, he is an unofficial neighborhood ambassador who regularly recommends its programs. |

| Seo-yun starts referring clients to the support-ive-housing program. | Clients seem ambivalent about their experiences and Seo-yun's attempts to connect with programs staff have left her unimpressed. She stops referring clients. A year later, she speaks poorly of the organization and has another supportive-housing partner she recommends. | The supportive-housing program seems to work well for Seo-yun's clients, and she connects with its programs staff to explore collaborations. Over time, they establish a more formal referral program and partnership agreement. A year later, the partnership is well-established and flourish-ing and Seo-yun's clients are benefiting. |
| --- | --- | --- |

This aspect of the mindshare equation might be expressed as:

**Engagement / motivation + time = mindshare**

Still, some organizations focus more on raising awareness and educating than on inspiring action. They believe that people lack information to make the right decisions, and that education alone will influence behavior. This theory is so prev-alent it even has a name: **information deficit syndrome**. But, as anyone trying to quit smoking or start an exercise program that will improve their health will tell you, understanding information isn't always enough to spark action. People are motivated to act by a variety of factors including religious beliefs, values, social norms, and others.

Communicating with a clear, consistent voice helps build mindshare by ensuring the organization's messages and visuals all support and reinforce each other.

In the article "Behavioral Economics and Donor Nudges: Impulse or Deliberation?" (*Stanford Social Innovation Review,*

January 15, 2019), authors Dean Karlan, Piyush Tantia, and Sarah Welch note that charitable donations are either *impulsive* ("quick gifts involving little analysis but rapid and positive emotional feedback") or *deliberate* ("thoughtful contributions that resist the temptation of fast, feel-good donor experiences and more deeply account for the recipient of the aid and its results").

The authors note six "nudges" for prompting impulsive giving:

- Make giving easy
- Make giving feel really good (immediately)
- Spotlight social norms
- Prime the right identity
- Emphasize different attributes
- Bundle short-term temptation with long-term benefits

And four different nudges for more deliberate giving:

- Create a commitment mechanism
- Set goals and make plans
- Leverage social norms and identity
- Bring attention to the choice

The emails, ads, posts, and other communications your organization sends to engage prospects, donors, clients, volunteers, and others likely employ many of these nudges. Communications teams experiment with new campaigns, segments, creative ideas, photos, copy, and other tactics to explore what works—some on an ad hoc basis, others through rigorous A/B testing. They use personas and mindsets to understand the people they want to reach and craft messages that will be meaningful for them. Ultimately, all of these strategies and tactics focus on building mindshare and engagement.

# UNDERSTANDING ENGAGEMENT FRAMEWORKS

Experimentation can teach your organization a lot about what motivates and sparks action in the people you're trying to reach. Sign-up forms with photographs of smiling kids have a higher completion rate. Weekend posts on social media are more widely shared. Each experiment helps your team get better and better at inspiring action. But how do you know you're focusing your activity and experimentation most effectively?

There are many theories about how you spark engagement in the marketing world and many frameworks to build on. Two of the most popular, the **ladder of engagement** and the **marketing funnel**, are regularly used by nonprofit communicators.

## Ladder of engagement

Donors, clients, activists, and other champions of your work today were once unfamiliar with your mission. Over time, they became aware of your work, started noticing or connecting with it, and began taking action. Perhaps they began that journey by signing a petition, attending an event, or clicking through from an email.

The ladder of engagement visualizes stages on a journey from the outside, where the people you're trying to reach are unaware, toward the inside, where they become supporters and advocates.

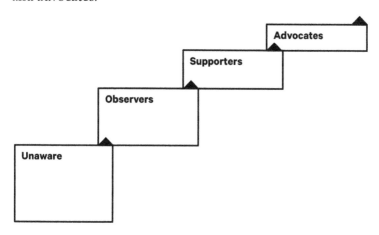

Each department in your organization has its own ladder of engagement. Fundraisers must acquire new donors, inspire them to make a donation, and then retain and grow their support over time. Programs staff must reach clients who will benefit from and participate, and engage them in other programs over time.

As your target audiences move up the ladder of engagement, build mindshare, and form deeper connections, the channels, tools, and tactics that are most effective often become more personalized. A first-time donor making a lower-level gift will likely receive a templated gift acknowledgment email or letter, while a major or sustaining donor will likely get a call or personalized note.

Effective communicators ensure they are inspiring the right people to connect and engage at every step in the ladder of engagement. Often, it's the primary responsibility of the marketing or communications team (particularly in a larger organization) to drive awareness and action at the bottom of the ladder of engagement and to collaborate with staff members in other departments to motivate action closer to the top, where connections generally become relationships.

Communications teams regularly use low-bar activities to spark impulsive actions at the bottom of the ladder of engagement. Care about climate change? Sign this petition! Concerned about animal testing? Share this message! Easy-to-do actions (follows, likes, etc.) don't always significantly advance the mission, but they may identify those who have the potential to connect in deeper ways. Communicators can spark more deliberate and ongoing engagement over time in order to move people toward deeper, more meaningful action.

## Marketing funnel

The ladder of engagement is typically expressed as linear and unidirectional, but people move up and down its steps over time. Someone who may have been loosely paying attention to your work might suddenly sign up, donate, and attend an event only to fade back toward inactivity a month or so later. Some marketing and communications professionals prefer to express the way their engagement is structured in more fluid terms, visualizing it as a funnel or vortex.

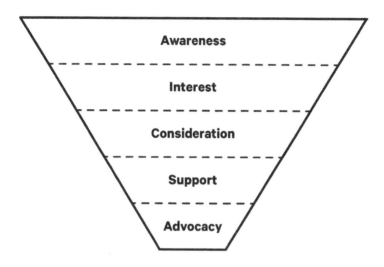

## Touchpoints

In his book, *What Customers Crave*, author Nicholas Webb maps five places a business interacts with its target audiences:

- **Pre-touch:** before they actually engage with you

- **First touch:** their first interaction with you

- **Core touch:** the majority of their interactions with you once they engage

- **Last touch:** the final interaction you have with them

- **In-touch:** the ways you stay in touch, providing lasting value

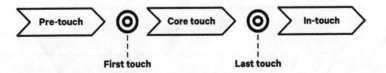

Pre-touch experiences are the ways you communicate with people who are unaware of your issues, work, or organization. Traditional marketing and outreach focuses here —on the efforts you make to reach and engage the unaware.

Because **first touches** are the experiences that welcome new people into your organization, they can strongly influence whether people act again or connect more deeply. Your organization's first touch might be an email received, an open house or gala attended, or the way intake is managed at the front desk. First touches are significant milestones on the road toward building mindshare and engagement. Webb's framework highlights their make-it-or-break-it role in many relationships.

**Core touch** moments are how nonprofits engage people who've already taken some other action. An organization's email, social media, and events may all be core touch communications.

**Last touches** are how you say goodbye or note the end of a key phase in a relationship. Some educational institutions and others use closing rituals such as graduation events to say goodbye to program participants. But how do you mark transitions for foundation funders or other donors whose gifts sunset, for a significant board member who will be stepping down, for a volunteer who's moving out of town, or for a client who's about to graduate from supportive housing? How does your organization celebrate transitions so the people you've helped (and who have helped you) are inspired to return and recommend—ensuring that they become lifelong advocates?

**In-touch** moments, the last of Webb's five touchpoints, reflect another important aspect of maintaining connections that's less obvious in the ladder of engagement or marketing funnel frameworks: how you keep in touch with people once they're no longer actively involved. In-touch moments maintain mindshare and help keep the door open, increasing the odds that people will someday reengage.

The ladder of engagement, marketing funnel, and touchpoints frameworks express engagement as if it has a clear beginning, middle, and end. In truth, engagement with a nonprofit more closely resembles a Chutes and Ladders game board, where people progress up and down in much less linear or predictable ways—influenced by how they engage and factors beyond your control.

Quantifying and measuring each stage, no matter which engagement model you use, will help you assess communications results. It can reveal where to spend more time, where you're most successful, and what happens when you try something new.

# BRINGING ENGAGEMENT STRATEGIES TO LIFE THROUGH TACTICS

A funny, smart, or moving social media post gets shared, promoting the organization and the sharer's desired public persona. An individual buys a ticket to a gala so their boss, the honoree, feels their support. All great relationships begin with connections: a simple exchange, transaction, or a need that is met. But many people want nothing more than a passing, transactional connection to a nonprofit that isn't one of their philanthropic priorities and may resent receiving communications that presume they are more committed than they really are.

Communicators test various tactics to learn what inspires interest and action. The marketer uses tactics that are the equivalent of chumming the waters at the bottom of the ladder of engagement in order to attract a lot of fish or putting out a lot of birdseed to attract a lot of birds. Some do so with clarity about the larger engagement strategy behind each tactic; others take a more ad hoc approach.

## Mapping tactics to strategy

The first connections made with an organization can be shallow, triggered by low-bar tactics like sharing on social media, signing a pledge digitally, or attending a free and convenient

STRATEGY 57

event. These impulsive actions are fast, simple, and easy for people to take, and they start to reveal who is willing to engage. Once an organization collects personal information such as an email address, phone number, or street address (which communications professionals call "converting") it can communicate proactively—using tactics that "pull" rather than "push" people up the ladder of engagement.

Effective communicators use various tactics to attract and engage a volume of people at the base of the ladder of engagement, accounting for attrition and segmenting messages so they reflect the audience's point of view as much as possible. They create easy, meaningful ways for people to connect (pledging, sharing, etc.) and conditions that inspire deliberate and deeper engagement.

Mapping communications tactics to an engagement framework illuminates mindshare and engagement in human-centered terms. Social media, for instance, can reach people who are unaware (those just outside the marketing funnel or ladder of engagement) and inspire them to act. Social media can also be used to build mindshare and keep in touch with people who are more engaged; it can be a useful core touch tool. Mindshare and engagement are easier to measure when expressed as ratios between lower-bar, more transactional tactics and deeper, more deliberate tactics. Here are a few examples of the kinds of ratios nonprofits might use to measure engagement:

- Two people opt in to receive email for every five new followers or likes on social media
- For every 100 people who opt in to receive our newsletter online, we acquire one new donor
- One out of 10 people who attend our annual spring clean-up volunteer event will become a sustaining donor
- For every 10 dollars spent on digital advertising we acquire one client

Attracting new people into your organization's ladder of engagement and inspiring them to take their first (perhaps impulsive) actions on your behalf is typically the primary focus of most marketing and communications teams. Higher up the ladder of engagement, the role of communications professionals in a nonprofit is often to support their colleagues in other departments. Somewhere in the middle, the responsibilities of communications and other departments gets blurred, requiring smooth interdepartmental and interpersonal collaboration. For instance, the development department will likely want to direct all communications with major donors—but they will need help from the comms team to produce materials.

At the Breast Cancer Research Foundation (*www.bcrf.org*), the Communications and Engagement Department sparks mindshare and engagement by generating leads with donors. They support corporate partnerships, coordinate events, manage media relations, and oversee a robust digital advertising program. BCRF's development staff focus higher up the ladder of engagement by cultivating and nurturing relationships with major donors.

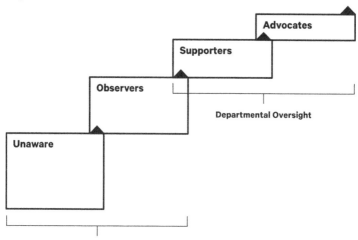

Runs, walks, and rides are transactional experiences for many participants that help form a connection to an organization or issue. Endurance athletes sign up to participate in a marathon or triathlon in order to gain access to the event, not necessarily because they are passionate about a mission. According to Blackbaud's 2016 Peer-to-Peer Fundraising Study, 24.9% of event participants will be retained by the organization, meaning that they see themselves as supporters of the mission and will participate in other activities, too—not just the event through which they connected initially. That means 75% of event participants show up just to run, walk, or ride in the race; they don't (yet) intend to support the organization in other ways. Communications staff and their colleagues in other departments (most likely, development or community relations) must collaborate to attract, retain, and engage event participants.

#GivingTuesday-focused communications are often used as a strategy to reach and engage people at the bottom of the ladder of engagement through impulsive transactions. Media around #GivingTuesday also reinforces mindshare with people farther up the ladder of engagement by reminding them of the organization's good work and asking them to publicly demonstrate their support.

Strong nonprofit communicators test out various tactics to see which ones are best at attracting, converting, and retaining.

## Campaigns: building mindshare and engagement through related tactics

Campaigns are related tactics designed to reach a particular audience and inspire them to take a particular action—often with a common theme, design, or other element. Effective campaigns weave together messages across channels and audiences, leveraging repetition to build mindshare and engagement.

Nonprofit campaigns invite people to pledge, donate, volunteer, vote, and share—becoming more deeply engaged with every action. They can also reinforce an organization's voice by leveraging its logo, tagline, visuals, and other brand elements.

Communicators regularly design and collaborate on campaigns that:

• **Recruit new program participants,** such as students, clients, and members.

- **Change beliefs, behaviors, and norms,** for instance, promoting positive behavior, destigmatizing something that's considered taboo, or changing public policy.

- **Raise money,** such as year-end or project-based fundraising appeals.

- **Raise awareness,** laying a foundation for behavioral change, giving, joining, or other actions higher up.

The Healthy Materials Lab is a program within the New School's Parsons School of Design (*www.healthymaterialslab.org*) that educates architects and designers about toxic building materials and provides them with the resources they need to design spaces that are healthy to live and work in. The Lab's awareness and recruitment campaigns leverage events, media awareness, social channels, and more to reach professionals who are unaware of the dangerous role toxic materials play in design and architecture. They also encourage visitors to learn why the use of toxic materials matters, sign a pledge, take a class, and more.

The Healthy Materials Lab's engagement strategy was conceived by its directors, Alison Mears and Jonsara Ruth, leveraging their small team's professional expertise, owned media, and Parsons School of Design's staff and students. It applies marketing best practices with its program's expertise and available resources, and has been successfully reaching and engaging its target audiences since its founding in 2015.

The campaign's creative theme, "Home is where the (harm) is," plays on the classic phrase "Home is where the heart is." Different headlines read, "Home is where the *perfluorooctanoic acid* is" and "Home is where the *trichloro-2-hydroxy diphenyl ether* is." Used in paid and owned social media, on the Lab's website, and elsewhere, the campaign was adapted for each channel to help reach and build mindshare with its target audience.

Multi-channel campaigns like the Healthy Materials Lab's "Home is where the (harm) is" communicate consistent messages across different media. In this case, the campaign is designed to raise awareness and change beliefs and behaviors, moving its target audiences (architects and designers) from being unaware toward selecting healthy materials when they design and build.

Campaigns also create a way for different groups and organizations to collaborate and gain strength collectively. Movements such as #MeToo, Black Lives Matter, and many health causes have all become bigger tents under which organizations and individuals can collaborate, combining forces for greater impact. Organizations with common agendas collaborate through campaigns to increase mindshare, engagement, and impact by pooling their resources and messaging consistently on a topic.

## Finite and evergreen campaigns

Campaigns can be finite (occurring within a limited time frame) or evergreen (ongoing).

**Finite** campaigns usually happen just once or very

occasionally, such as a special fundraising appeal when the board chair retires, an awareness campaign to educate peer organizations about a new program, or a particular external event (such as an election). Finite campaigns have a clear beginning, middle, and end.

**Evergreen** campaigns are designed to reach and engage on an ongoing basis, over an extended period of time, or at the same time each year. For example, a community center runs a recruitment campaign each spring to encourage neighborhood parents to sign their kids up for summer camp, or an advocacy organization recruits activists for its annual legislative event.

Many nonprofit communications teams develop a calendar with a steady rhythm of evergreen and finite fundraising, awareness, recruitment, and other campaigns designed to attract, engage, and maintain mindshare.

## Acquisition campaigns

Acquisition campaigns strive to reach and engage people who are unaware—those currently outside an organization's ladder of engagement or marketing funnel. They inspire new people to take an action that engages them in your work while giving you an easier or less expensive way to communicate with them directly in the future (most often, by getting their email address). Acquisition campaign strategies include a measurable objective for conversions—the number of people who "convert" (from being unknown to known) by providing their email address. When new people convert, they are no longer strangers to your organization. They've engaged by taking an action, and you've gained the ability to communicate with them directly.

Many people feel that providing their email address to an organization is like lowering the drawbridge and inviting the cavalry to storm the castle. Effective acquisitions campaigns rely on personally meaningful and easy-to-take, low-bar actions that don't involve much risk or spark second-guessing. Acquisition campaigns can fail if people are asked to take an action that exceeds their comfort level or commitment to the issue, or if they don't get something meaningful in return.

A small California farmers' market with one full-time employee was struggling to build a list of people who regularly visited the market so it could promote special events and test out fundraising. The employee regularly walked around the market asking people to share their feedback and inviting them to sign up to receive e-news. People offered their feedback willingly, but few gave up their email address. The employee needed something more motivating. What would be worth giving up their email address for? She brainstormed ideas with her board and local partners, finally landing on the idea of providing special recipes online that could only be accessed once a shopper gave the market their email address. Want the recipe for your local favorite restaurant's signature dish? Sign up for the farmers' market e-news and receive insider access. This simple and elegant acquisition strategy helped the organization build an email list inexpensively by offering its target audience something in exchange for their email address.

When a nonprofit has a department called "marketing" (rather than "communications") it is usually focused on acquisitions as its primary mandate. Marketing departments are also more likely to design campaigns that leverage paid media. They create ads that promote exhibitions at museums, events at community centers, membership in cultural institutions, and more.

Designing evergreen and finite acquisition campaigns, launching and running them, measuring the results, and adjusting future campaigns to get stronger results can be time-consuming and complex work, requiring specialized skills and deep expertise. Generalist communicators responsible for designing and executing significant acquisitions campaigns will likely need mentoring and professional development to become effective acquisition-campaign strategists and executors.

## Engagement and renewal campaigns

For better or worse, many people take their first action on behalf of an organization or issue impulsively. Perhaps they signed up, pledged, or donated because something inspired them to *in the moment*, not because they're committed to supporting the work. They gave the farmers' market their email address only because they wanted the free recipes, or they donated just because their friend asked them to.

Whether or not the team that manages acquisition campaigns is called "marketing" or "communications," it must collaborate closely with peers in other departments to inspire newly acquired donors, clients, members, and others to remain engaged and move up the ladder of engagement or more deeply into the marketing funnel. At a minimum, they'll send regular email updates and other communications. They may also explore other ways to expand mindshare, engagement, and renewal collaboratively.

Events are often a key relationship builder at the top of your ladder of engagement, inspiring *supporters* to become *advocates.* They become even more effective when preceded by and followed with other mindshare- and engagement-building experiences. Perhaps every person who attends the gala hears more about the speakers through other communications they receive post-event. Everyone who attended the open house might receive a series of follow-up communications thanking them and suggesting additional action, like a conversation with one of your programs staff. However it happens, engaging the newly acquired and inspiring them to keep your work in mind and take further action is central to growing the lifetime value of the people who support your mission.

The Metropolitan Museum of Art (*www.themetmuseum.org*) offers three levels of membership, each with different prices and benefits. Its membership department acquires new members in many ways, including a campaign called "Members Count," which features special offers such as early access to see special exhibits. Benefits increase at higher levels of membership, layering in perks like access to a private dining room, reciprocity at other museums, and more. The Met provides museum visitors with reasons to keep visiting and renewing (or deepening) their support.

According to the Fundraising Effectiveness Project (*www.afpfep.org*), fewer than half of all first-time donors make a second gift[2]. Reaching and engaging people who have converted and inspiring them to renew their support requires different tactics than acquisition campaigns do. If your fundraising team's objective is to reactivate lapsed donors, a successful campaign plan will marry their interest areas with the tactics that will most effectively engage them, blending the expertise and insights of both departments (development and communications).

## Developing campaigns

Remember "Conjunction Junction"? "This is your brain on drugs"? "The mind is a terrible thing to waste"? Great campaigns share an enduring theme, story, or message that can be woven throughout earned, owned, and paid media channels. They introduce an idea or narrative that's personally relevant and meaningful to the audience they target, distilling the essence of the message into something memorable and effective.

Many successful campaigns are developed after research (formal or informal) illuminates what the campaign's primary audiences want, think, and do. A written brief (see "Essential communications planning," below) is often developed before research and perhaps refined afterward. This short document clarifies the campaign's target audience, actions, and success

2    *www.afpfep.org/reports*

metrics. It can be used to get everyone on the same page and keep them there over time by documenting and clarifying what you set out to achieve.

Campaign concepts—the overarching narrative for the campaigns—are developed next using insights from research and the brief as inspiration. How will the campaign look and sound? What visuals and copy will it use? Map out campaign tactics, timing, and budget—ideally before the campaign launches and implementation begins—so the path ahead is clear.

Some of the most memorable campaigns use unexpected strategies to cut through the clutter and grab attention. They are catchy (like Schoolhouse Rock!), surprising (like the ice bucket challenge), shocking (like Kony 2012), funny (like the Great Schlep), or moving (like Love Has No Labels).

# MANAGING EXPERIENCES

When Kathryn Glass joined the YMCA of Greater New York (*www.ymcanyc.org*) as its senior vice president for marketing and communications, she embarked on a project to learn about members' experiences. She dropped in to various Y locations to observe how members used them and asked for input on their pre-touch, first touch, and core touch experiences with the Y. While most marketers think in terms of outreach and campaigns, Glass identified other touchpoints that offered critical opportunities to move prospects and new members up the ladder of engagement, such as making the voice mail system easier to navigate or improving how staff greeted visitors when they walked through the door. To improve retention and grow membership, Glass focused on improving several touchpoints, using the Y's brand to ensure clarity and consistency in the organization's voice, so every member's experience feels integrated and seamless from start to finish.

Expert nonprofit communicators like Glass understand that growing mindshare, creating engagement, and communicating with a clear voice require coordination across departments. They must collaborate to develop content, capture, convert, and engage audiences—creating positive experiences and touchpoints at every step. They plan and implement a mix of strategies and tactics that move target audiences up a ladder of engagement.

This collaborative approach is a different way of working than is typical in a for-profit corporation or political campaign, where marketing departments have a high degree of autonomy and, in some cases, fewer audiences. Engaging donors, clients, volunteers, and activists without coordinating with the people who lead those departments is significantly more challenging.

Client experiences are also managed differently in the for-profit sector. Larger companies often have customer service departments to assess experiences and address complaints. They use call centers, Net Promoter Scores, and dedicated staff to connect the dots and smooth out the bumps. Busy Trader Joe's locations have dedicated people who help manage the lines, reducing customer frustration and confusion. Car rental companies encourage employees to come out from behind the counter and shake hands, greet customers personally, and introduce themselves with a smile. But nonprofits rarely have staff dedicated to customer service who can afford to create and institutionalize core touch moments like these.

At the NPNext conference in 2014, Steve MacLaughlin, vice president of data and analytics at Blackbaud, proposed that the head of communications and the head of digital or IT at nonprofits should join forces, creating a new position called chief experience officer (CXO). He argued that online experiences are so central to a person's experience of a nonprofit that they shouldn't be overseen by an IT professional, web manager, or a less-than-senior staff person. A CXO can also assess offline experiences, as Kathryn Glass did at the YMCA of Greater New York, using them to improve communications at multiple levels.

The CXO (or others in the communications department) works closely with fundraisers to understand and help improve a donor's experience with the organization. They also lead the communications or marketing department. They develop strategies and tactics (for instance, email schedules, newsletter content, etc.) designed to move people up the ladder of engagement. They ensure the organization has a coordinated communications calendar and that all metrics are tracked and compared to past performance and industry benchmarks, then used to optimize future work.

This person is also responsible for proactively defining an organization's brand, which exists in the eyes of internal and external constituents. They can help shape the organization's brand strategy, visual identity, and messaging platform. They can train staff to write, speak, and design "on message" so an organization speaks with a clearer, more consistent voice. They can save time and money by coaching new hires and external communicators on how to communicate most effectively. They might measure levels of mindshare and engagement, using those insights to sharpen messages and inform department-specific work, such as with donors, activists, or clients.

When the experience of an organization is inconsistent, unmanaged, or poorly executed, donors, clients, members, and others may be unaware, uninterested, unclear, or unengaged with its work. It's like *Groundhog Day*: starting over from scratch every time. But when the experience of your nonprofit is managed successfully, donors, clients, policymakers, and other target audiences form a more successful connection or relationship to it.

# ESSENTIAL COMMUNICATIONS PLANNING

Plans define what we will do and what we hope to achieve. Effective nonprofit communicators walk a delicate line between proactively planning and leaving room to react to shifting external and internal forces. They set communications goals and objectives that support the organization's vision, mission, and goals (typically articulated in its strategic plan or annual operating plans). They regularly measure results and review plans to keep them top-of-mind and course-correct when needed.

There are four essential planning tools for most nonprofit communications teams:

- **A department mission statement:** What is the mission or mandate of communications as a function? What departments or aspects of the organization's work does it primarily support? Having a departmental mission statement can help ensure staff spend the majority of their time working in service of the right things.

- **An annual department plan:** The communications department should set its own annual goals and objectives informed by the organization's strategic or operational plans.

- **An external communications calendar:** Mapping out the email, campaigns, and other external communications the organization will produce throughout the year avoids a wealth of challenges.

- **Project briefs:** Capturing the goals, objectives, strategy, tactics, and assets for significant projects in writing will get everyone aligned from the start and serve as a framework for decision-making at key junctures.

## Department mission statement

What areas of the organization's work are most important for communications to support? What does it exist to do as a department?

In 2015, the small in-house communications department of Good Shepherd Services (*www.goodshepherds.org*) audited the communications needs of the organization and its capacity to meet them. With more than 1,200 staff members across numerous departments distributed throughout New York City, speaking with a clear, consistent voice externally and keeping staff up to date about the organization internally proved consistently challenging. At that time, only two people worked in the communications department. They frequently struggled with the discrepancy between the organization's goals for its own visibility and the reality of what such a small team could produce. A departmental planning session produced a mission focusing on facilitating internal communications.

The organization's leadership and communications staff acknowledged that they needed clearer strategies and tactics to empower staff people in other departments so they could spearhead more external communications, which led to a process of focusing communications activities and expectations at Good Shepherd Services.

Organizations with more communications capacity and staff typically have broader departmental missions. Some even publish their communications department's mission online, such as this example from Princeton University (*www.princeton.edu*):

*The Office of Communications promotes and protects Princeton University's reputation of excellence.*

*We manage the main University website and social media channels, the content and design of the University's official print publications, the release of University news, media relations, and the use of Princeton's name and image.*

*We work with offices and departments across campus to tell Princeton's story to a wide range of audiences around the world, and we work collaboratively to provide a variety of communications services to faculty and staff.*

*We are committed to creating communications that engage and inform various audiences and that promote the University. Our in-depth knowledge of the University and communications strategy enables us to help shape messages so they are best understood by their intended audiences.*

This mission statement expresses the desired outcomes

of engagement and communicating with a clear organizational voice. It also stresses the importance of collaboration with other departments and their own professional expertise as a team.

A departmental mission statement articulates what communications exists to do and can serve as a useful guide when limited resources have to be allocated and decisions made.

## Annual planning

Managers and director-level staff in a nonprofit organization or other business typically work at two levels: *in* the business and *on* the business.

While the majority of time will be spent working in the business on a day-to-day basis, taking time out to reflect on the business and set annual plans can help ensure communications is effectively working toward the right goals and objectives.

The following questions can help identify an organization's greatest communications strengths and opportunities for growth:

- What can communications do to support the organization's goals and objectives this year?

- What goals and objectives do other departments have that communications should support?

- Do we have the capacity we need to achieve our goals as a department? If not, what can we realistically do to improve our capacity this year?

- Are we well-informed about who our audiences are, how they perceive our organization, and how their experiences engaging with us currently are?

- How might we grow mindshare and engagement with them this year?

- How might we assure that our organization is speaking with a clear and powerful voice?

- How might we improve the experiences people have when they interact with our organization?

- How might communications become more sustainable and less dependent on key people organization-wide?

- What will be most important for our department to achieve this year given our resources?

Annual communications plans are often developed at half-day or daylong retreats, then captured in a simple document that may be as brief as one page. Displaying them visibly along with the department's mission can help keep them alive and referenced, as will reviewing them at least quarterly.

## Communications calendars

Communications calendars are specific and tactical; they outline external communications plans for email, mail, and other owned media. Often developed in spreadsheet format, they map which channels and themes will be used to communicate—detailing events, holidays, and other variables that impact what is sent.

A communications calendar includes organization-wide and department-level communications. It can identify:

- Key events or initiatives to promote that will generate mindshare and inspire action

- Campaigns and themes that tell a cohesive story across all channels and reinforce the organization's voice

- Tactics used to communicate and their frequency

- Outcomes needed for each department to reach their objectives

| | Q1 | | | Q2 | | |
|---|---|---|---|---|---|---|
| | JANUARY | FEBRUARY | MARCH | APRIL | MAY | JUN |
| | WHERE THERE'S A Y, THERE'S A WAY | | | SPRING INTO SUMMER | | |
| | WHERE THERE'S A Y, THERE'S A WAY | LOVE YOUR HEART (TBD) | BUILDING COMMUNITY | HEALTHY FAMILY FUN (TBD) | SPRING INTO SUMMER (TBD) | SUMMER |
| -GLANCE: ing and Doing | 1.) The Y helps people find their way through health & fitness. 2.) Winter Membership Campaign. 3.) Promote new YMCA weight loss program. | 1.) The Y helps people find their way through friendship, connection, and love. 2.) Run a member engagement activity. 3.) Promote heart healthy classes. | 1.) The Y helps people find their way through community. 2.) Provide programs that build community. 3.) Promote your branches local communities. | 1.) The Y helps families find their way through health and fun. 2.) Highlight healthy, Kids Day. 3.) Promote other special family/youth programs. | 1.) The Y helps people find their way through health, fitness, and summer run. 2.) Run special fitness classes to get in shape for summer. 3.) Promote water safety. | 1.) The Y helps p identify and the 2.) Participate Periods of play instru 3.) Promote swim progra |
| Marketing | January Membership Campaign | Summer Camp Promotion | Summer Camp Promotion | Summer Camp Promotion | Summer Membership Campaign, Summer Camp Promotion. | Summer Members Summer Camp |
| Internal Communications | My Y newsletter (email) | My Y newsletter (print & email) | My Y newsletter (email) | My Y newsletter (email) | My Y newsletter (email) | My Y newsletter |
| Public Relations | Where There's a Y, There's a Way | Love Your Heart (TBD) | Building Community | Healthy Family Fun (TBD) | Spring Into Summer (TBD) | Summer |

*The communications team at the YMCA of Greater New York, which helps coordinate communications for 26 local Ys, maps quarterly themes and connects them to each department's specific needs in their communications calendar.*

- Communications calendars provide a level of detail and structure that can also inform:

- Weekly campaign progress reports to identify if specific campaigns are on track to meet their objectives

- Monthly meetings with senior-level communicators and other department leaders to discuss what's happening and report on progress against approved plans

- Quarterly department plan reviews and adjustments

- Sharing communications results organization-wide or with other departments

- Annual planning for communications

There are many free downloadable templates and useful articles on how to produce a communications calendar available online.

## Project briefs

One of the simplest and most effective ways to build strategy into any project or campaign is to draft a project brief. In the design world, these are often called **creative briefs**, although their utility extends far beyond creative projects.

A useful brief articulates a project's goals, objectives, strategies, and assets, capturing details necessary to ensure that the team doesn't lose sight of what it's trying to achieve. For many projects, a simple one- or two-sentence brief will suffice. It can be as basic as:

"Our goal is to reach _____ (audience) _____ and inspire them to _____ (action) _____ in order to ____ (result) _____. We will do this by ____ (approach) _____."

For example: *"Our goal is to reach newly diagnosed patients and their care partners and inspire them to download and use our 'Conversations with your Doctor' guide at their next doctor appointment in order to ensure that patients are better informed by providing them with questions they might not otherwise know to ask. We will do this by promoting this guide across all of our owned, paid, and earned media."*

Bigger projects or those that continue over long periods of time may involve more assets, systems, and members of your team. Capturing the complexity of what you're working with, including key assumptions, in a project brief can keep everyone on the same page along the way.

Articulating S.M.A.R.T. (specific, measurable, achievable, realistic, and time-bound) objectives in the brief can help identify the data points that will be most important to collect and measure. The goal in the example above might be measured by the number of downloads of the "Conversations with your Doctor" guide, and by surveying people who downloaded the guide to find out if they used it and if it affected their plans and treatment outcomes.

A project brief also provides a tangible way for communications staff to collaborate with their peers in development, programs, and advocacy. It keeps everyone aligned by providing a document that can be revisited consistently throughout the project (ideally, brought to all meetings, reviewed at regular intervals, and treated like a reference checklist or guide), ensuring the project and its team across all departments never stray from the path.

## Flexible plans

Most organizations need to plan for the unexpected, too. Nonprofits that are significantly influenced by current events or news cycles can't always plan too far in advance, and must allow bandwidth for shifts that will inevitably come up. They plan for and create "anchor" content (a percentage of stable, predictable content they can produce in advance), and leave room for the unexpected. An advocacy organization working on a timely issue, for example, may plan only 30% of its communications calendar in advance in order to leave the majority of the calendar free for responsive content shaped by the news, changes in policy, and other external factors that will unpredictably emerge. Many organizations also share content from peers and partners.

In November 2016, on the heels of the general election, the ACLU (*www.aclu.org*) published a letter to President-Elect Donald Trump in *The New York Times* outlining and challenging several of his campaign promises. This letter, rapidly produced and placed by the communications team within a matter of hours, positioned the ACLU as a leader of the resistance at the start of Trump's presidency. That, along with other efforts the ACLU communications team initiated and launched, helped exponentially grow the ACLU's membership, visibility, and fundraising support.

Drafting project briefs and communications-specific calendars takes time staff may feel they do not have. But without them, it's easy to lose sight of what matters most and difficult to identify what went wrong. They provide a framework to ensure external communications are proactively building mindshare, sparking action, and expressing the organization's voice clearly and deliberately.

# CHAPTER 3

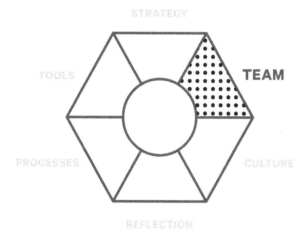

STRATEGY

TOOLS

**TEAM**

PROCESSES

CULTURE

REFLECTION

"Talent wins games, but teamwork
and intelligence win championships."

~ Michael Jordan

## WHY THE TEAM MATTERS

Building the right communications team is essential, particularly as a nonprofit transitions away from being founder-led. Who should an executive director hire as they build the department? Into what roles? What skills will be most valuable to grow mindshare and engagement, communicate with a clear voice, and build sustainable momentum?

# HOW MOST COMMUNICATIONS TEAMS GROW

Founded in 2006, Charity: Water (*www.charitywater.org*) leveraged digital tools and high-design communications from the start. The organization's communications were immediately eye-catching, innovative, and effective in attracting big donations from tech giants and support from coveted younger donors.

Its founder, Scott Harrison, who had previously worked as a promoter and photographer, inherently understood the power of strategic communications to advance his organization's mission. Charity: Water's first employee was hired for programs expertise and the second was a designer with brand-building chops. The internal communications team played a central role from the start in growing the organization into an individual-donor fundraising powerhouse. Two years after its founding, the organization generated more than $6 million in annual revenue, and by 2012 it was consistently raising north of $30 million annually. It's often referenced as a "household name" nonprofit: one many people have heard of and perhaps engaged with.

Most nonprofit founders don't have Harrison's experience cultivating the spotlight to build mindshare and engagement, nor would they be comfortable leaning into communications and brand identity as a growth strategy. It's more common for communications to lag behind other areas (programs, development).

Startups and other small organizations rely on the founder or CEO to manage communications much as Harrison did, with their own voice serving as a surrogate for the organization's. As the nonprofit grows, communications functions are absorbed by other people or departments with other primary functions. Board members or volunteers manage runs, walks, rides, galas, or other events. Government relations staff design and launch advocacy campaigns. Development staff write year-end fundraising appeals. Few see themselves as "communicators," although this work creates and sustains the mindshare and engagement that advances the mission. But because these other departments prioritize their primary functions, the communications work may be underserved.

When communications functions are decentralized and dispersed across departments, the organization's voice lacks an internal champion responsible for expressing it clearly across all departments. Without a clear voice, building mindshare and engagement is harder. Staff and board members begin to feel frustrated that the website and other external communications don't feel consistent, connected, or clear. External audiences see the organization in a more siloed way. A donor or activist may get an email asking them to sign a petition (sent by the programs team) followed by another on the same day asking them to make a donation (sent by development), with no coordination on messaging, language, or timing. Donors may not see the reasons why they should support the whole organization, clients don't know there are other programs they might also benefit from, and so forth. It's during this stage that staff often complain that they aren't "speaking with one voice" as an organization and the idea of hiring dedicated communications professionals often emerges.

In addition to a desire to communicate with a clearer voice and increase output, hiring dedicated communications people also happens in most organizations once the operating budget and staff are big enough to warrant centralizing and hiring new (non-programs or development) staff. Nonprofits with missions that require proactive recruitment and outreach hit this point earlier than others, but often not until their annual operating budgets exceed $1 million.

Membership, arts, events-driven organizations, and community centers (like a Y or JCC) are typically an exception to this pattern. They must build mindshare and engage the right audiences early in their organizational life on a larger scale. They establish a communications or marketing department sooner because they recognize it's essential to the success of their programs; they can't survive or thrive without it.

The first dedicated communications person (hired specifically for a communications job) is often tasked with creating materials for external outreach, fundraising, event promotion, and more. If they are a good writer, designer, and project coordinator, the organization's communications benefit quickly, and others who've been doing this work (probably not as well) start to experience relief. The expanded capacity this new comms hire provides makes it easier to produce a greater volume of external communications.

The communicator's day fills up fast with the mechanics of maintaining social media, sending out email and newsletters, and updating the website. As budget allows and results emerge, most organizations then hire additional communications staff to supplement this person's capacity. They add people with complementary skills or augment what can be produced in-house by hiring external specialists, often to manage channels that require extra attention. They have titles that point to the channels and tactics driving the majority of their work: website manager, social media specialist, media relations manager, and so forth.

The communications people initially hired to work in other departments may migrate into a stand-alone communications team designed to support the entire organization, or they may continue to be "embedded" in development, programs, or other departments. Regardless, all organizations want a communications team that's large enough to support their efforts effectively without unnecessary overhead.

## STRUCTURING FOR SUCCESS

Suzanne Shaw, the director of communications at the Union of Concerned Scientists (*www.ucsusa.org*), has led her department through several phases of significant growth in order to meet the needs of the organization. At the start, Shaw hired people with specialized skills and built a communications department with writers, designers, multimedia experts, and other capacities. But the larger the team got, the more Shaw noticed new gaps and challenges, so she hired a consultant to help her examine her team's skills and structure.

As in many other organizations, the people in Shaw's department had job titles emphasizing tactics and channels (social media manager or email specialist), not outcomes or results (engagement manager). Shaw also identified that her team needed specialists with strong project management skills, not just the ability to write, design, and produce effective communications.

Shaw began the process of reorganizing her department into two teams: content creators and engagement managers.

**Content creators** are writers, designers, multimedia artists, developers, and other people who have the interest and ability to produce materials. They are experts with particular technical skills and are highly focused on the craft and quality of their work.

**Engagement managers** produce and manage interactions designed to move people up an organization's ladder of engagement. They may be experts in particular channels or tools (for instance, social media, email engagement, or marketing automation), and may or may not also have content creation skills (most likely writers). Their greater strength, however, often lies in project management, ability to collaborate, and capacity to get things done. As director of the department, Shaw was responsible for planning, analysis, and managing priorities.

Restructuring the communications team at the Union of Concerned Scientists into content creators and engagement managers helped leverage existing strengths in roles that played more naturally to their passions and skills. It also provided the Union of Concerned Scientists with a structure that could scale as the organization continued to grow.

In smaller organizations, communications staff are expected to be both content creators (usually writers) and engagement managers. Generalists able to effectively manage multiple projects, collaborate affably, and produce materials independently are highly valuable and successful. Unless the mission requires particularly deep subject matter expertise or the CEO sees communications as an essential program (as Charity: Water's founder did), writing, design, video, and other content creation expertise is often outsourced to freelancers.

In larger organizations with bigger communications teams such as the Union of Concerned Scientists, content creation and engagement roles are more likely to be separated and specialized as staff with greater expertise are hired to meet the volume of work. Bigger nonprofits are typically able to hire writers with subject matter expertise to produce publications and edit content. They might hire data scientists who conduct tests to learn what sort of language or visuals produce better open, click-through, and response rates, or multimedia experts who can produce podcasts, videos, and other content in-house.

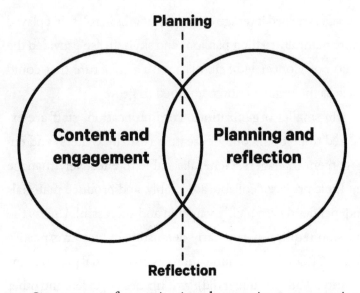

**Planning**

**Content and engagement**

**Planning and reflection**

**Reflection**

Some types of organizations have unique communications needs that require hiring for specific content creation
or engagement skills earlier. When an organization's subject
matter requires a particularly strong level of fluency in a specific topic, having in-house people who can write and edit
accurately can become essential. This is frequently true with
scientific content, issues that have significant political or other
complexity, or with a model so innovative that describing the
work clearly requires insider expertise. Advocacy organizations, whose missions center on changing people's hearts
and minds around an issue or influencing legislators, often
require in-house subject matter expertise or media relations
mastery, whereas organizations whose communications teams
exist largely to support fundraising or grassroots community
engagement often prioritize digital engagement expertise.

Organizations whose subject matter does not require deep expertise or training often benefit from hiring communicators with engagement-oriented skills sooner than content creators. This type of employee can effectively write a plan or a brief, work well with their colleagues in other departments to understand their priorities and deadlines, create a project plan, and make sure the right people are doing what's necessary to get the job done. Their ability to listen, develop, test, and learn as they communicate with external audiences will come in handy internally, too, when they collaborate with peers. Content may be created by writers, designers, and other experts working on a freelance or voluntary basis or by staff members in other departments who are themselves content experts. Even the largest organizations don't staff for all their content creation and engagement needs; they hire essential talent and outsource other work, particularly periodic or finite projects.

The most difficult communication function to outsource is the internal coordination, management, and maintenance required in daily communications work: following up with a peer in another department to get their edits or feedback on an article about the program in the newsletter, consolidating comments from the leadership team on a new brochure, or checking that an email was sent to the correct list of recipients. Hire staff with strong project management and relationship skills first so they can keep multiple projects moving and build sustainable momentum. Outsource content creation (to freelancers, volunteers, or agencies) initially until you can afford to grow your team in-house and it's clear exactly how much work you'll have for them to do.

Thinking differently about job titles can also help structure a communications team for success. Someone with the title "social media specialist" will see their expertise and their role as managing social media. But if that person's title shifts away from the channel they predominantly work in toward the outcome they are striving to achieve and becomes "community engagement specialist," they may view their job—and priorities—differently.

Consider titles that point toward *outcomes* rather than *channels* to connect your communications team more directly to their role in advancing your mission. This will encourage them to focus on results, not channels or tactics, and to feel empowered to try something new that might make their work more effective.

## Integrated versus standalone teams

Should you integrate communications staff into other departments or build it into a separate department? Where communications sits within a nonprofit's structure affects employee satisfaction and how clear they are about their department's mandate.

In 2016, the Nonprofit Marketing Guide (*www. nonprofitmarketingguide.com*) conducted a survey of 1,613 nonprofits in which 39% of respondents claimed they worked on an integrated team, defined as "marketing and fundraising working together on an equal level under the same manager." Thirty-seven percent of nonprofits described their communications teams as separate with equal authority within the organization.

While the percentages of both team structures is basically the same, there are important differences. Integrated teams are much more likely than separate-but-equal teams to feel direct responsibility for meeting both fundraising and community building/engagement goals. Job satisfaction is also significantly higher among staff on integrated teams.

"Nonprofit staff on integrated teams where marketing and fundraising staff work together on an equal level under the same manager were four times as likely to say they felt directly responsible for fundraising goals as those working on separate teams with different managers," says Kivi Leroux-Miller, the author of the report. "Members of integrated teams were twice as likely to feel responsible for community building and engagement goals."

If your communications team exists predominantly to build mindshare and engagement with donors and prospects, consider integrating it into development. If the group exists to expand client outreach and recruitment, consider integrating it into your programs team.

## Marketing versus communications

The American Marketing Association (*www.ama.org*) defines

marketing as "the activity, set of institutions, and processes for creating, communicating, delivering, and exchanging offerings that have value for customers, clients, partners, and society at large."

In the nonprofit sector, the word "marketing" is typically used to describe teams that are responsible for recruiting people into programs. A nonprofit's marketing department might be responsible for conducting outreach to inspire people to visit a museum, attend a film series, or join the community center. Marketers typically focus their area of responsibility on the bottom of the ladder of engagement or the entrance to the marketing funnel.

In larger organizations, marketing is often a separate department from communications, although the work these two departments lead will have substantial areas of overlap and require strong coordination.

"Communications" is more commonly used as an umbrella term including marketing functions and other work such as internal communications oversight, brand management, and more. Communications encompasses all the practices of creating and sustaining mindshare and engagement that help advance the mission.

Standalone communications departments may be better equipped to form a connective tissue between all of the organization's communications. They are more likely to be represented on the leadership team and able to influence the organization's culture of internal and external communications. Because they are separate from but equal to other departments they have a greater ability to create and encourage the use of brand assets that help the organization communicate with a clear, consistent voice.

## HIRING EFFECTIVE COMMUNICATORS

Chandra Hayslett, the director of communications at the Center for Constitutional Rights (*www.ccrjustice.org*), began her career as a journalist. Her nonprofit career started in 2010, and was interrupted by a two-year stint in a communications agency, where she learned to work with a broad mix of clients and gained new technical skills. The Center for Constitutional Rights' CEO Vince Warren hired her in 2017 to help bring an updated vision for the next era to life, counting on her to jump in fast, proactively plan, strategize, and lead the communications team.

Hayslett's hands-on experiences as both a nonprofit communicator and journalist equipped her to manage staff pragmatically, roll up her sleeves and do the work herself when needed, and work with limited resources and tight timeframes. Within weeks, staff in other departments commented that she'd already improved the Center for Constitutional Rights' communications. Within a year she'd successfully overseen an organizational rebranding, the launch of a new podcast, and many other successful projects that grew the Center's engagement with new activists and supporters and sharpened its voice.

Every nonprofit leader hopes they'll hire someone who's as good a fit for their organization as Chandra Hayslett—but it can be difficult to get it right, especially for CEOs with little background in communications. Many nonprofit leaders don't know what type of expertise will be most essential as they consider applicants. Looking to advance strong employees, they promote underqualified people in other departments who've demonstrated some communications capacity—such as a programs staff person with strong writing and editing skills, or a development person who's good at project management. Executive directors hire people from the corporate or political sectors hoping they will bring some of the acumen from those sectors into the organization.

But both can be problematic. People with no experience running complex communications projects or managing teams often struggle with a steep learning curve. Those new to the nonprofit sector typically struggle to adjust to the limited resources, lack of financial metrics, and politics that are standard in most organizations. As they struggle to find a groove, their peers and colleagues start to become doubtful of their capacity, handicapping their odds for success.

So who should an executive director hire?

A 2016 survey conducted jointly by Big Duck and Nonprofit Marketing Guide, "What It Takes to Be Great: The Top Five Factors of Successful Communications Teams" (*www.bigduck.com/insights/5-factors*), identified five elements that helped successful communications teams thrive.

They are:

• Expert staff

• Clear focus on limited priorities

• Strong internal communication

• Creative experimentation

• Supportive leadership

The strongest communications teams are anchored by expert staff: people who've already worked in another non-profit's communications department, ideally in senior-level roles. The more complex or specialized the mission, the more valuable subject matter expertise is, too.

An individual who has worked in a successful nonprofit marketing or communications department already has relevant experience in building mindshare and engagement. They arrive with useful digital, print, media, or other skills. They've ideally worked in an organization with a clear voice and understand how that's achieved, or at least see why that's an important communications strategy. They understand what building sustainable momentum within an organization's communications team means because they've experienced how many details slip through the cracks on projects with no processes and continuity. Their odds of diving in fast, working with no or very limited budgets, and navigating internal politics are probably greater. Bonus points if they also have an agency background where they've been trained to work proactively, juggle multiple clients, conduct research, test, and get buy-in.

Hiring a communications leader who has worked in communications roles within peer organizations also increases the chances that they will come with a wealth of ideas, subject matter expertise, and best practices they can use to hit the ground running. Often, mid-level employees looking for advancement are excited for the opportunity to step into a more senior role and build a department.

## Key skills for top communicators

For communications to flow internally throughout the organization and externally to the right people, peers and colleagues must trust and respect top communicators' ability to transform their ideas and needs into effective messaging. Communicators, perhaps even more so than their peers in other departments, must demonstrate maturity and skill to earn the respect and trust of their colleagues. When staff are more junior, less skilled, or just downright difficult to work with, it's going to be a challenge to spark the deep collaboration you'll need to achieve strong results. This ability to work well with others reinforces a culture of sustainable momentum: one where everyone contributes constructively to communications.

The most effective communicators bring passion, positivity, perseverance, and patience to their role. Their passion for the mission and positivity make them likable and relatable. Perseverance and patience give them the tenacity necessary to work with others and overcome obstacles.

Building communications infrastructure also requires real alignment between the communications team's director and the CEO. The leader of the organization must have confidence that the leader of the communications function understands their vision, direction, and primary audiences. Without this trust, the CEO will be tempted to get overly involved in the department's work.

Creating sustainable momentum in the department also requires discipline, systems thinking, and strong management skills. In fact, strong project management and planning skills in the first and most senior communications people may be more beneficial than creative expertise. Writing and design (content creation) can often be sourced from other staff members or freelancers, but planning and ensuring projects stay on track typically cannot. First and foremost, a communications staff person must assume accountability for the overall execution of communications no matter how large or small their team is.

Expert communicators at organizations of all sizes strive to build a bench of people who can write, design, speak, and share, along with "back office" tools that define the systems the organization uses. The organization's communications will hum along once this infrastructure exists because it's not dependent on one person's talent, skills, or institutional knowledge.

## Finding creative ways to staff a comms team

Christine Hughes was the director of institutional giving and science programs at Weill Cornell Medicine (*www.weill.cornell.edu*)

for many years. With close to 100 people staffing various development, marketing, and communications positions within external affairs, she was a part of a large team with terrific resources available for producing fundraising communications. In 2017, she accepted a new role at Burke Neurological Institute (*www.burke.weill.cornell.edu*) as its vice president for advancement and was tasked with building an integrated fundraising and communications team entirely from scratch.

Hughes hit the ground running building her integrated fundraising/communications department. She began by developing an overarching strategy that helped her identify the skills that would be most essential for her new department's success. Grounded in a clear vision for communications, she reached out to various consultants and other experts she'd worked with successfully over the years who had the skills she knew she'd need but couldn't afford in-house yet, inviting them to collaborate on an hourly basis. Each consultant agreed to provide Burke with 10 hours a week of their services and participate in a weekly team call. Within weeks, Hughes had assembled her own part-time freelance dream team.

In time, Hughes created in-house positions for key functions, and adjusted the working group of consultants she'd assembled to meet Burke's changing needs. Despite having a much smaller budget, staff, and overall team, Hughes built a successful structure and sustainable momentum quickly and effectively.

## MEASURING YOUR COMMUNICATIONS TEAM'S ROI

In larger organizations, major gifts officers are highly paid employees responsible for managing a portfolio of major donors. They have six-figure salaries and generate seven- or eight-figure or even greater levels of revenue for their organization. The return-on-investment (ROI) for a major gifts officer is clear and measurable.

But the ROI of communications staff and their efforts is less obviously measurable. So how do you assess the value your organization receives from this team? And how much should you invest in communications in order to grow your organization? Unfortunately, this is much harder to assess.

At its most basic level, communications is a function necessary to the operations of an organization, just like HR or finance. You can't really do business without it. Many communications responsibilities (producing collateral, for instance) are also categorized as programs or education expenses on the balance sheet, making it more challenging to see what the department truly costs the organization.

"Table stakes" for communications in an organization of any size should be the ability to consistently and reliably produce the basic tools necessary to build mindshare and engagement with key audiences, express the organization's voice, and maintain a degree of sustainable momentum. If your team isn't able to achieve some acceptable level of those three communications outcomes, it's possible you've got the wrong people or not enough capacity.

When the communications function becomes a bigger investment, for instance as the department grows in size or budget, the standards for the value it must provide also scale up. A strong communications director will develop annual plans for their department using the organization's larger goals and the CEO's vision and input as a guide. Where possible, they might articulate measurable objectives that can be used to more accurately define success. Here are a few examples.

| Organization's Annual Goal | Communications Objectives | Communications Outcome This Supports |
|---|---|---|
| Launch new program for senior citizens, filling first two cohorts with qualified participants. | Establish a list-building program that will generate 250 qualified participants by June. Collaborate with programs team to recruit 60 qualified participants into programs. | Building mindshare and engagement—*programs* |
| Expand major gifts efforts and close $250,000 in gifts from new major donors. | Start segmenting major donors in database consistently. Launch a program that automates segmentation of donors and tracks their digital behaviors, generating leads for development team. Produce new communications campaign and collateral with development team. | Building mindshare and engagement—*fundraising* |
| Increase our organization's visibility in the community. | Benchmark current visibility. Pilot targeted visibility campaigns using paid and donated media, measuring results. Use insights to design sustainable visibility campaign. Present to leadership. | Clear voice (this strategy focuses on traditional marketing techniques) |
| Increase our organization's visibility in the community. | Benchmark current visibility. Sharpen our organization's brand strategy and messaging. Train all staff on messaging and being effective ambassadors. Integrate training into HR and develop ongoing practice forums. Develop and implement a plan to leverage staff proactively as brand ambassadors in the community, measuring results. | Clear voice, sustainable momentum |

Most strategic plans can be parsed down to annual goals that can be supported by communications. Setting measurable objectives like these will illuminate how your communications team helps advance the mission.

# CHAPTER 4

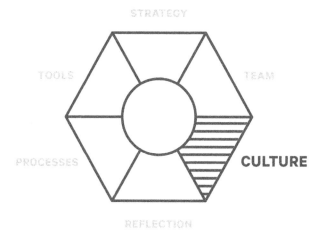

STRATEGY

TOOLS

TEAM

PROCESSES

CULTURE

REFLECTION

"We don't see things as they are.
We see them as we are."

~ Anaïs Nin

## WHY CULTURE MATTERS

Culture is the lived expression of the organization's values and the label we use to describe the norms that are considered acceptable within an organization or group. Culture is "how we do things around here"—and it is learned and established through small-group interactions.

In *The First 90 Days*, a popular book about managing a transition into a new organization or different job, author Michael D. Watkins explains that every business has a "shadow organization," which he defines as "the informal set of processes and alliances that exist in the shadow of the formal structure and strongly influence how work actually gets done." This is culture in action.

Achieving successful communications outcomes requires productive collaboration within your organization; the beliefs, attitudes, and mindsets of everyone on staff can have a profound impact on how they work together and what they achieve.

If your organization isn't communicating well internally, it's probably not communicating well externally, either.

# DEFINING WHAT'S ACCEPTABLE (AND NOT) IN AN ORGANIZATION

After a few weeks working with an education organization that hired Big Duck to help with their messaging, my staff noticed a pattern. The nonprofit's C-suite staff, a smart group of seasoned professionals, rarely talked in front of their boss. Instead, their executive director dominated every conversation, often expressing frustration or airing complaints. We attempted to draw out others and encouraged them to share their opinions, but the staff would answer tentatively or not at all if their boss was in the room. After meetings ended, people inevitably lingered behind or called us later. They shared their opinions and substantive ideas more candidly in these sidebar conversations, and often didn't align with their executive director's views. The first five minutes of these exchanges would be devoted to the airing of their frustrations about working with him, and the last five spent determining what was worth trying to do given how difficult he was, and what should just be set aside because it wasn't worth the fight. The staff clearly wanted to see the work advance in directions that they felt powerless to achieve.

That team's ability to contribute substantively was stifled by the environment the executive director was creating. Several people told us that the only way to survive in this top-down culture was to form private alliances (often with board members), hide projects from the executive director, and follow his vision strictly when working directly with him. Great people left often, moving on to environments that valued their contributions more. Others stuck it out because they loved the mission, and just tried to keep their heads down and pick their battles carefully.

Support for their work had plateaued. A peer organization was growing exponentially—raising much more money and expanding its programs rapidly—in the same community. Everyone but the executive director saw this as a byproduct of their inner dysfunction. It was obvious why this group was struggling to grow their programs and fundraising engagement: This organization's executive director was creating a culture that held people back from doing their best work.

An organization's leadership sets the culture deliberately or accidentally by establishing patterns for acceptable behavior. Staff observe what management considers acceptable and operates within those norms. Are achievements, innovation, and successful results celebrated and rewarded? Are bad behaviors tolerated?

Since communications staff must collaborate with other people and departments, their ability to build mindshare and engagement is deeply impacted by the organization's culture. An environment with collaborative, welcoming norms sets a positive tone for interdepartmental work and individual exchanges, just as an office that maintains silos and celebrates autonomy can make it harder for staff to collaborate.

## How we do things around here

Remember the last time you started a new job? If you are like most people, you anticipated what your first day would be like and felt a little nervous about it. Would your new coworkers be welcoming? Who would show you the ropes? What would be appropriate to wear or to say in your first meetings?

Perhaps you relaxed and felt at ease when a number of people stopped by to introduce themselves and share a tip on your first day. Maybe you were assigned an office buddy who showed you around and whispered in your ear, helping you navigate how things are done. Or, if you worked at the organization I referenced earlier, your colleagues might have begun conspiratorially offering advice to avoid conflict with the executive director, encouraging you to keep your head down and establish back-channel ways of getting things done. These behaviors are all expressions of the organization's culture. We can't always see it, but we feel it deeply—and it sets the tone for how work gets done.

When Cindy Robbins became the chief people officer at Salesforce, she began a number of initiatives designed to elevate the voices of women within the company and reduce "bro culture." Together with Salesforce CEO Marc Benioff, Robbins embarked on a number of culture-shifting projects, including "Women Surge," an initiative that required 30% of quarterly meeting attendees to be women. "As an officer of the company, it has given me permission, when I'm in certain meetings, if there are 15 people around the room and I'm the only woman, to say to the organizer of the meeting, "Why am I the only woman in this meeting?'" said Robbins in an interview with CNN's Poppy Harlow[3]. "I do that because I think we've created this culture now, where it feels like it's permissible to say that."

## How communications is perceived within your organization

Aspects of the organization's overall culture are apparent in how departments like development, communications, and HR, which largely exist to support the goals of other departments, are viewed and treated. Is every department and team member valued and respected? Who holds power?

Examine the racial and gender hierarchy that influences communications too. "Many organizations have racialized and gendered divisions of labor, with people of color concentrated in support positions," notes Rinku Sen, writer and senior strategist at Race Forward (*www.raceforward.org*). "This amounts to a segregated, inequitable workplace, which can create cultural and power-related tensions within an organization."

Fundraisers often strive to create a "culture of philanthropy" within their organizations—an attitude that fund development is healthy, positive, and valuable. What if your organization were to establish a healthy "culture of communications?" All staff would view communications as intrinsic to the success of the organization overall, and collaboration might improve.

---

3     *www.cnn.com/2018/12/24/success/boss-files-salesforce-president-cindy-robbins/index.html*

## How culture helps set priorities

The American Friends Service Committee (AFSC) (*www.afsc.org*) is a Quaker organization that promotes lasting peace with justice as a practical expression of faith in action. Mark Graham heads up its communications team, which collaborates with other departments to help advance the mission. During a communications department retreat, Mark set up an exercise sparked by a blog post he'd read by Kivi Leroux-Miller (*www.nonprofitmarketingguide.com*) titled "Comms Department Like a Drive-Thru Window or Reservations Required?" To help the group identify the culture surrounding their work, Mark asked his team, "If our department were a type of restaurant, what type of restaurant would we be?"

At first, the staff was divided. Some felt they'd be a high-end, top-tier establishment. They regularly lead projects with strategy, conduct research, and execute most projects at an exceptionally high level. Others felt they'd be a fast food restaurant because they churn out some projects fast, prioritizing speed when necessary.

In the end, they agreed that they would be a four-star restaurant with a high-quality (but very fast) food truck. This metaphor allowed Mark's team to differentiate between the projects that communications just has to deliver fast and the projects where there is time (and perhaps other resources) to plan and execute more methodically. AFSC's culture supports the communications team's capacity to be both a strategic and a tactical resource rather than pigeonholing them into one category or role, which helps them advance important projects even when they aren't always urgent.

|  | **URGENT** | **NOT URGENT** |
|---|---|---|
| **IMPORTANT** | **Quadrant 1** Urgent & Important | **Quadrant 2** Not Urgent & Important |
| **NOT IMPORTANT** | **Quadrant 3** Urgent & Not Important | **Quadrant 4** Not Urgent & Not Important |

In *The Seven Habits of Highly Effective People*, Stephen Covey maps out the matrix illustrated above. Covey notes that many day-to-day activities become urgent but may not be truly important (quadrant 3). Despite that, people often spend time in the urgent quadrants and end up neglecting the important quadrants. Fixing a broken website or donation form is an important and urgent (quadrant I) tactic. Communicating with an audience you are trying to build a relationship with (perhaps next-generation donors) is important but not urgent. A/B testing or experimenting with a new platform can also be important but not urgent.

Some organizations, particularly advocacy groups or others that work in areas that are affected by current events, have cultures driven by working reactively. Everything feels urgent, so it becomes hard to distinguish what is truly important. This, too, can normalize reactive communications and make it difficult for other less urgent (but useful or important) projects that might ultimately be more valuable to make progress. Communications teams in these organizations are great at producing things fast—a press release, statement, or report—but struggle to establish the processes and tools that might make communicating easier in the long run.

Establishing an organization's clear voice as a strong brand involves many important but not usually urgent tactics. If the culture of communications leaves no room for pushback or control from the team, they'll spend most of their time on the urgent (responding to requests) at the expense of the important.

## How leaders shape culture

Big Duck regularly facilitates daylong brand strategy sessions for our nonprofit clients. In advance of those meetings, I often have a preparatory call with the CEO of the organization to talk about the day's agenda, the attendees, and the team's dynamics. CEOs who are sensitive to their own role shaping their organization's culture describe how they strive to create and maintain a healthy culture through team participation. They'll deliberately hold back their own opinion until the end, encouraging others to share first, or they may prefer to make decisions based on the majority. One nonprofit CEO I spoke with recently noted her desire to elevate the voice of a new staff person and asked that we help create experiences that give that individual a chance to speak up or lead. She was proactively thinking about how this meeting could be used to establish this person's important role in the organization—and deliberately shaping culture by doing so. CEOs are better positioned than most people in an organization to shape a culture where others' voices are valued, and to manage, with sensitivity, the often outsized power and influence of their own voice.

In his article "Leadership Can Shape Company Culture Through Their Behaviors" (*Harvard Business Review* 2016), Jim Whitehurst, CEO of Red Hat and the former COO of Delta Airlines, wrote, "One of those elements [of an innovative culture] is a willingness to have open and frank discussions about what separates great ideas from bad ones. If you want to be innovative, you also need to accept failure. If our associates aren't pushing boundaries and sometimes failing along the way, we probably aren't pushing hard enough. But by accepting and even celebrating a failed effort, we promote innovation. We will reward someone who tries to climb the tallest mountain, even if they fall short of the summit, because they have created an experience we can learn from and build upon. That's what innovation is all about."

Leaders build communications-friendly, healthy cultures by establishing clear organizational values that encourage positive and productive interpersonal working relationships. They use practices like those used at Red Hat that transform these values into meaningful interactions, shaping how people interact with each other in conscious ways that establish healthy organization-wide norms, and carefully use the power of their voice.

The beliefs, attitudes, and mindsets of everyone on staff can have a profound impact on how people work together and, as a result, how successful communicators will be at achieving their goals. Maximize the communications team's value by clarifying the department's primary mission or mandate organization-wide and empowering them to push back or seek other solutions to help colleagues prioritize the right work at the right time.

## Values that unite, motivate, and empower

Values are guiding beliefs and principles. When expressed clearly and used deliberately, values can help establish a healthy culture by providing language that can label behaviors and suggesting how the group can strive to work together. This helps everyone—not just the people responsible for communications—collaborate more effectively.

Wayfinder Family Services (*www.wayfinderfamily.org*) is a large human services organization based in California with multiple locations and programs. Its culture stems from a set of common values expressed on its website:

### Inclusive

*We honor the fundamental value and dignity of all individuals. We strive to create a culture in which everyone is accepted and encouraged to fully participate.*

**Empathetic**

*We seek to develop a deeper understanding of our children and families. We work to embed empathy into our decision-making, interactions, and actions.*

**Collaborative**

*We can't do it alone and we must do it together. We work in partnership to address the holistic needs of children and families.*

**Whatever it takes**

*We never give up. We will always be there for our children and their families.*

**Innovative**

*We are agile and forward-thinking. We continually seek out better ways to help children and families thrive.*

**Driven**

*We take every opportunity to move forward in our strategic direction and to create meaningful change.*

Wayfinder's values elevate the importance of hard work, inclusivity, and tenacity. These core beliefs might be particularly useful when hiring, and they also help communications staff encourage peers to dig in and collaborate deeply on interdepartmental projects.

The National Brain Tumor Society (*www.braintumor.org*) formally articulated its organizational values as part of its 2018 strategic planning process. They are:

**Patients first**
*We are fiercely committed to providing a voice and community for all impacted by brain tumors.*

**Best-in-class science and service to our community**
*We adhere to rigorous standards across our scientific and community initiatives.*

**Relentlessly results driven**
*We set aggressive goals, achieve measurable results, account for our work, and accurately report our progress. We drive positive change and have the courage to disrupt the system and take risks to achieve our goals.*

**Constructive, candid and transparent**
*We practice fearless candor by being honest, accountable, and transparent in all that we do.*

**Committed to public trust**
*We are prudent stewards of donors' funds and conduct our organization openly, operate efficiently, and communicate frequently.*

**Collaborative and inclusive**
*We believe that working with others is critically important to achieving our mission.*

**Positive (can-do) attitude**
*We believe a positive attitude is essential for achieving our goals.*

The National Brain Tumor Society's values encourage behaviors it feels are important for the staff and board to use internally such as candor, transparency, achieving results, and collaboration. Other values such as "best-in-class science and service to our community" guide behavior both internally and externally.

When values are explicitly articulated, they provide a starting point for difficult conversations and a way to celebrate and reinforce positive behaviors. They can also help determine how to resolve conflict or determine a path forward when there are multiple options. Using these values as guidelines, a staff or board member of the National Brain Tumor Society might begin a conversation with a peer they are in conflict with by saying, for example, "Because our values encourage us to practice fearless candor by being honest, accountable, and transparent in all that we do, I want to raise an issue concerning how we're working together."

But using stated and shared values to open up challenging or difficult conversations is not always realistic; power dynamics, bias, below-the-line behaviors, basic competency issues, and other challenges may override even the best intentions. It's hard and risky for a staff member to confront a difficult supervisor or executive director, no matter how clearly an organization may have articulated their shared values.

## Defining and living your values as an organization

Defining your organization's values requires exploring questions such as:

- What do we stand for or against?

- Which behaviors do we reward? Which are unacceptable?

- How do we communicate internally and externally?

- What beliefs are so central to this place that, if absent, people would quit or leave?

For organizational values to truly be shared and used as a set of behavioral guidelines—an informal contract of sorts—true participation, understanding, and buy-in are critical. Everyone needs to have skin in the game.

At UTEC (*www.utecinc.org*), an organization that works with disenfranchised young people in Lowell, MA, values are actively integrated into the physical space as a reminder of their centrality. They are painted on walls, worn on T-shirts, and integrated into conversations at all levels.

**UTEC is a family.** *We* **assume goodness** *behind everyone's actions. We show* **mad love,** *unconditionally accepting each person. We offer everyone a* **clean slate,** *never giving up. We carry out* **respectful curiosity,** *always seeking out moments to connect.* **We are sponges,** *actively seeking feedback. We embody* **contagious passion** *in all we do.*

**UTEC is a catalyst.** *We* **think big** *about what we can achieve. We continually* **chip away,** *demonstrating relentlessness in our pursuit of positive change. We* **plant seeds of peace** *and cultivate trust. We see* **beyond the mask,** *knowing there's always more beneath the surface. We* **ignite social justice.** *And we* **spark sustainability**—*for our young people, our enterprises, and our physical environment.*

Integrating values into UTEC's programs so visibly and dynamically throughout the organization has helped them become more than a tool to shape internal communication and culture; they are an effective programs tool, too.

Values-driven organizations integrate them into HR practices such as hiring, performance reviews, and more. Great leaders model their organization's values consistently in what they say and do—or what they *don't* say or do. That means addressing bad behavior directly, celebrating wins, and keeping the values alive, visible, and regularly referenced.

Developing values is a multistep process. In-house communicators may guide this process and bring its results to life if they have the right facilitation skills and internal support.

It begins by bringing to light your teams' shared values through inclusive conversations. Once ideas are on the table, they can be combined, edited, and refined. Get the ideas right before focusing too much on language; this can take several rounds of discussion and revision.

Integrate your organization's stated values internally (perhaps through visible expressions around the office and in HR practices such as hiring and training), and express them externally (on your website, brochures, and other organizational collateral).

To keep your organization's stated values alive, review and discuss them regularly (perhaps annually) with staff, so any concerns or shifts are resolved collaboratively. Develop exercises and spark conversations that accentuate, articulate, and reinforce your organization's values more frequently at all levels of your organization—from on-the-ground programs to board meetings. Set targets and create spaces to help you assess your progress. Celebrate your organization's values in action whenever you see them, labeling and mirroring examples others can learn from and follow. Proactively shaping a healthy culture may help reduce burnout, establish positive norms for new employees, and keep your organization's values healthily pulsing through your organization's bloodstream.

# CHAPTER 5

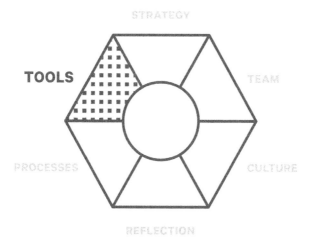

"Start where you are.
Use what you have.
Do what you can."

~ Arthur Ashe

## WHY TOOLS MATTER

Mateo was the associate director of external affairs at a large organization with a strong communications team. He had helped build the department, established a healthy culture, and operationalized processes that supported their efforts to reach and engage target audiences. Mateo worked on the organization's brand over time, coached everyone on staff to write and speak on message, won awards for various campaigns, and spoke at conferences about the team's exemplary work. The organization had gone from being a "best kept secret" to a relatively well-known leader in its area and had grown significantly. When a smaller organization approached Mateo to become its first-ever director of communications, he leapt at the chance to tackle new challenges.

Mateo kicked off his new job by conducting an audit. He asked the senior leadership team about their needs and expectations for communications, assessed existing resources, reviewed current assets and systems, and analyzed past results using industry benchmarks for comparison. He shared his findings with senior leadership and articulated a new vision for how communications could help the organization advance its mission. Mateo identified key audiences, developed a powerful messaging strategy, and proposed staffing changes to meet capacity. The executive director was delighted and gave him the green light to get to work.

Mateo saw that before he could move forward with his new initiatives, he had to shore up the foundation of what was already happening in his department. His first six months were busy with activities such as streamlining the production of the organization's e-newsletter, replacing a lackluster freelance copywriter, figuring out where all the passwords were, and more. In parallel, he worked on a plan to bring his vision for communications to life. It detailed several new campaigns, updating the organization's database and other digital tools, and starting a blog and video series featuring expert staff members.

But new barriers emerged as Mateo launched each new initiative. There were no consistently used visuals or messaging that could be integrated into campaigns and other content. Each department maintained its own email lists and used different software. And, of course, budgets and staff time for communications were limited.

Mateo maintained an open dialogue with the executive director and managed expectations. They both wanted to see communications evolve into a strong department that helped the organization grow, but there was a lot of work to do before it would have that capacity. It would take some time.

It's often the case that experienced communications professionals like Mateo find they have to create or improve their organization's basic tools for communicating. Just as a chef needs ingredients to work with, so too does a communicator. The first step—assessing what's working, what's missing, and what seems to be broken—is necessary in order to prioritize and move forward realistically.

Communications leaders need a toolkit that contains **brand assets** that combine to create a compelling story—via print and digital content—about the organization and its work. That **content**, disseminated through the right **channels** to reach the right audiences, builds mindshare and engagement, communicates in a clear voice, and creates sustainable momentum. And we can't overlook other key resources in the communications mix: **time** and **money**.

As you read the sections in this chapter, consider scoring your organization's tools on a scale of zero to 10 to identify your greatest gaps or opportunities for improvement.

# BRAND ASSETS: TOOLS FOR SUCCESSFUL COMMUNICATION

The definition of branding has changed dramatically since its origin on the cattle ranch, as has the nonprofit sector's understanding of its relevance and usefulness in advancing the mission. Today, mission-driven organizations increasingly recognize that differentiating themselves is important in order to build mindshare. *Branding* has become synonymous with *perception*—a term that distributes responsibility between the organization that's communicating and the audience who receives and interprets those communications.

An organization shapes perceptions by communicating deliberately, consistently, and strategically with a clear voice. That doesn't necessarily mean changing the brand. For many organizations, great progress can be made by simply being more consistent and deliberate when creating materials and experiences. Nonprofits need a suite of specific brand assets that everyone uses to communicate—including a brand strategy, visuals, and messaging—codified in a written guide.

In 2017, Burke Medical Research Institute formalized its affiliation with Weill Cornell Medicine and hired new leadership, including a director of external affairs who was tasked with building its fundraising and communications capacity. The timing was right to redefine its brand assets. First, leadership completed strategic planning, redefining the organization's vision and mission, and changing its name to Burke Neuro-logical Institute.

**Vision:** *Hope demands innovation and brilliant science, and every day with our academic affiliate, Weill Cornell Medicine, we transform groundbreaking research into promising neurological treatments. Our specialized clinics (called quaternary care clinics) will revolutionize the therapeutic pipeline—speeding up the process of turning insights from the lab into life-changing results for patients with neurological impairments.*

**Mission:** *We are a research institute dedicated to finding cures for chronic neurological disabilities. We transform groundbreaking research into clinical treatments so that people can see, talk, and walk again.*

Next, they honed the institute's brand personality and po-sitioning—its brand strategy. A new brand guide documented the updated brand assets; accompanying training helped both existing staff and new hires understand how to use them in communications.

**Positioning:** *We work together to bring desperately needed sci-entific breakthroughs, hope, and cures to people with neurological disabilities.*

**Personality:** *Visionary, big-hearted, brilliant, relentless.*

Burke Neurological Institute's leadership began hiring, fundraising, and communicating with this rearticulated voice.

## Primary brand assets

There are three key brand assets that form the building blocks of consistent communications: *brand strategy, visuals,* and *messaging.*

### Brand strategy

A **vision statement** articulates what a nonprofit organization is working toward and its **mission** defines how it will get there. A **brand strategy** translates that vision and mission into how the organization wants to be understood by its target audiences. There are many models for brand strategy ("brand purpose," "brand promise," "value proposition," etc.), many of which can be useful. Brand strategy models reduce complex notions about your organization to a simple expression of who you are, providing a road map your team can consistently use to express your organization's voice.

In my book, *Brandraising: How Nonprofits Raise Visibility and Money Through Smart Communications* (Jossey-Bass, 2010), I outlined a process of developing a clear and cohesive organizational identity and communications system that supports the organization's mission (called "brandraising"). Nonprofits should define their unique **positioning** (the single idea they want to be known for in the minds of their target audiences) and their **personality** (the tone and style they will use to communicate). Positioning and personality together create a powerful brand strategy that nonprofits can use to create more consistent communications that help them speak with a clearer voice.

A brand strategy defines how everyone should communicate when they write, speak, or design on behalf of your organization. It helps your staff and board objectively answer questions such as "Does this speech reflect our organization's voice?" "Which new website design best communicates our organization's brand?" "Is the design and copy in our year-end fundraising on strategy?"

**Visuals**

Most people will simply skim through a website, email, newsletter, or other communication they receive from you, so how your materials look can be just as important as what they say. Consistent use of the same logo, colors, fonts, and types of images helps your communications feel cohesive—presenting a unified appearance for the organization.

Developing a new identity is typically a fun creative process. It's an opportunity to capture through design what people love most about the mission and to work with creative professionals that most nonprofit staff people rarely get to collaborate with. Afterward, most staff are delighted to abandon a stale visual identity in favor of something that feels fresh, relevant, and future-focused—especially when they had a hand in crafting it. Big Duck's 2013 study of the impact of rebranding on nonprofits, "The Rebrand Effect" (*www.bigducknyc.com/insights/the-rebrand-effect*), showed that providing staff with a more compelling suite of visual elements to work with quickly improved morale and correlated with other positive outcomes.

At the end of a rebrand, most designers create a style

guide or brand guide, which defines rules for using the new visual identity correctly. It includes details such as how the logo should and should not be used, what colors, fonts, and other images should be used, and more. A thorough guide makes it easy for anyone producing materials on your behalf to design consistently on brand. It's shared with any staff, freelancers, or other partners who create communications materials.

**Messaging**

While only a handful of staff within a nonprofit will design materials, just about everyone will write and speak on behalf of the organization at some point. Giving them clear messaging will help ensure that your organization's voice is clear and consistent.

**Messaging** is an overused term that means many different things in the nonprofit sector—and has no one-size-fits-all definition. Most importantly, messaging should be scaled appropriately for your organization's capacity and fully integrated into your team's workflow so they routinely write and speak from the script.

The Chinese-American Planning Council *(www.cpc-nyc.org)* is the largest Asian American social services agency in the United States. In 2017, it employed more than 5,000 people, yet it didn't have a single dedicated person responsible for communications. Without a guide to help them speak with a consistent voice, most people in the organization could explain their program's or department's work, but they struggled to tell a larger, more comprehensive story about the agency overall.

When CPC received a grant from the Robin Hood

Foundation (*www.robinhood.org*) to develop messaging, it started at the beginning: with a clear brand strategy and a straightforward and comprehensive way to explain the organization's work. The messaging was structured simply so all staff could learn and remember it without significant effort.

In other organizations, *comprehensive* messaging can be less useful than *persuasive* messaging, which is designed to help an important and specific audience (donors, clients, policymakers, perhaps even a specific segment or mindset) understand the work and take action.

A nonprofit organization's messaging assets might include:

- A tagline that works well with its name
- Compelling vision, mission, and values statements
- Comprehensive messaging: boilerplate language and/or an "elevator pitch" that provides a high-level overview
- Persuasive messaging targeting specific audiences (e.g., donors, clients, members, advocates)
- Fundraising case for support
- A stirring manifesto that can be used as a general rallying cry

Along with visual assests, compile messaging elements into a brand standards guide that you use both as a training tool and an ongoing reference manual for all employees. To further build support and compliance, consider empowering a "brand coach" who can advocate for the brand internally.

There are many great resources on branding (including many free articles, ebooks, and videos online at *www.bigduck.com*), and no one right way to rebrand. The key is to pick one approach or model that feels appropriate for your organization and implement it consistently.

Review your organization's brand assets (brand strategy, visuals, and messaging) after a significant shift in organization strategy or leadership to ensure they are still relevant. If not, staff and board members will avoid using them and perhaps create their own, which can have a fracturing effect on a nonprofit's voice. If necessary, adjust the brand assets to align with your current strategy.

Bake your brand assets into your HR practices so new staff members are trained to use them from the start. By training all new staff and coaching existing employees to write, design, and speak "on brand," you'll turn everyone into an ambassador for your organization, which amplifies your voice and helps create sustainable momentum.

## Ambassadors: when people are brand assets

Some organizations align themselves with spokespeople and ambassadors who become associated with the organization's brand. They are brand assets too, albeit finite ones.

Geoffrey Canada was an educator who was appointed president of the Harlem Children's Zone (*www.hcz.org*) in 1990. (It was called Rheedlen Centers for Families and Children at the time; Canada rebranded and renamed it later, and also became its CEO.) Under his leadership, the organization transformed education and opportunity for the children who live in Harlem, creating a new model and inspiring *U.S. News and World Report* to name him one of America's Best Leaders in 2005.

Like many nonprofit leaders, Canada had a vision for his organization. But he's also a compelling communicator who knows how to express his vision in ways that connect with the hearts and minds of others, garnering attention and support from people well beyond the community in which he worked.

Canada transformed and grew the organization as its leader while also serving as its spokesperson. He was profiled or featured over a 10-year period in *The New York Times, The New Yorker, 60 Minutes, the Oprah Winfrey Show, Late Night with Jimmy Fallon,* and other prominent media outlets. Outside of New York he became immediately recognizable when American Express aired a commercial during the 2010 Academy Awards that featured Canada and the Harlem Children's Zone.

Powerful spokespeople like Geoffrey Canada often have an instinct for how to tell a story that elevates their organization's profile with a consistent voice. If you're lucky, some of them already work within your organization or serve on your board. Armed with clearly defined messages, they become assets that your organization can leverage to reach and engage the right people.

Like Geoffrey Canada, Sister Paulette LoMonaco, executive director of Good Shepherd Services (*www.goodshepherds.org*), was of a legend in New York City. As a member of a religious community, Sr. Paulette may not appear to be a powerhouse leader and fundraiser at first glance, which is perhaps part of why she's so effective. Under her direction, Good Shepherd Services grew into one of New York's largest and most powerful human service organizations, with more than 1,200 staff people and more than $88 million in annual revenue in 2016. Her compelling vision and ability to communicate it, often in entirely unexpected and unassuming ways, are why many New Yorkers who know her use terms such as "secret weapon," "stealth fundraiser," and "powerhouse" to describe her.

While Geoffrey Canada and Sister Paulette LoMonaco approach their roles as spokespeople and ambassadors differently, both are clearly assets their organizations have leveraged to expand their active pipelines and express their voice.

Other organizations cultivate or stumble upon celebrity connections. Celebrity spokespeople, particularly those who've developed strong social media followings, can drive more traffic to a website than a feature article in a major media publication might. But be careful before hitching your organization's wagon too closely to a celebrity's platform.

When an organization is closely associated with one person (the founder, executive director, or other key spokesperson), the individual's and institution's identities intermingle. This may tarnish an organization, as Jason Russell's public breakdown in 2012 impacted the organization he founded, Invisible Children (*www.invisiblechildren.com*). Leveraging individuals as brand assets for specific, short-term projects (rather than as the sole face of the organization) can make it easier for the organization to weather a retirement, departure, or scandal.

# CONTENT: CREATING A COMPELLING NARRATIVE

Nonprofits increasingly rely on content—the story of the organization's mission, the people and causes it benefits, its work locally or globally—to build mindshare. **Content** is a broad term used to describe the expression of ideas across various channels. It is expressed and shared many ways: long-form, editorial-style narratives and short social media messages; digital newsletters and printed brochures; messages that you share and those that others share on your behalf.

Content helps staff celebrate the positive results of their work, shows funders what their investments achieve, and helps constituents understand why they should avail themselves of an agency's programs and services. Producing and posting digital content online regularly is also critical to elevating a website's visibility by leveraging the technology that determines its search engine rankings.

## Translating brand assets into content

An effective brand strategy defines what an organization wants to be known for and how it will express its voice. Asking questions such as "Does this piece of content reinforce what we want to be known for?" or "Does it support our positioning?" helps determine what content to prioritize and provides a strategic way to reject something that's out of alignment with the organization's voice.

Earlier, we reviewed Burke Neurological Institute's brand strategy:

**Positioning:** *We work together to bring desperately needed scientific breakthroughs, hope, and cures to people with neurological disabilities.*

**Personality:** *Visionary, big-hearted, brilliant, relentless.*

Imagine two stories that have been submitted for publication in Burke's newsletter or blog. The first tells the story of a patient who has been able to walk again as a direct result of new technologies and medicines created at Burke. The second describes a scientist's research over the past year into how stimuli impact specific areas of the brain. Both stories exemplify Burke's mission of finding breakthrough cures, but the first story's emphasis on the human implications of the work is more aligned with Burke's brand strategy, so it would be more appropriate to feature or prioritize when shared publicly. Perhaps the more scientific story could be edited to support Burke's brand strategy by adding a section about the future treatments this lab work will lead to and how they will benefit patients. Burke's content editor might also encourage adjustments to the way articles like these are written so they express the organization's personality more clearly, such as adding language that feels big-hearted.

## Producing content

Nonprofits are widely staffed by smart, passionate, mission-driven experts who can effectively blog, write, and speak about the work. Communicators project manage and edit to help produce quality, consistent, on-brand content that builds mindshare and action. Many struggle to get their colleagues to produce articles, videos, and other content regularly. Some are great thinkers and writers, able to express themselves powerfully with little help and in minimal time, while others slog through even the most basic assignments. But when an organization becomes dependent on one or two key people for content (often, the executive director or head of programs), it becomes harder to distribute the work and build sustainable momentum.

Organizations that commit deeply to sharing their thought leadership as a key content strategy—such as the Wildlife Conservation Society (*www.wcs.org*), Union of Concerned Scientists (*www.ucsusa.org*), or the ACLU (*www.aclu.org*)—hire dedicated content creators who can help consistently write, edit, shoot, design, and post. Smaller or less resourced teams focus on producing content for fewer channels sustainably, often created by the same team that produces everything else.

Many organizations share content they don't produce themselves by reprinting (with permission) articles written by peer organizations, sourced in the news, and more.

Expect a robust content platform to consume a significant percentage of the communications staff's time (perhaps

10%–50%), and some amount of other staff's time, too. Content is a hungry beast that needs to be constantly fed. Encourage your team to generate extra content before they begin to post anything publicly so you have a backlog of work you can post as needed. Posting regularly and consistently is key to the success of content marketing, so don't commit unless you have the capacity to produce content several times a month, if not weekly.

# CHANNELS: GETTING YOUR MESSAGE OUT THERE

How do you learn about new issues or organizations? Read about them online or in the paper? Hear about them on the radio or from a friend? Communication channels are abundant today, and many of them are inexpensive or free, creating a glut of choice. So how does an effective communicator prioritize?

All of the options boil down to three types of channels your organization can use to develop its active pipeline and express its voice:

- Channels you directly control, otherwise known as **owned media**

- Channels you don't control, or **earned media**: the coverage your organization receives when other people highlight your work in their own channels

- Channels you pay for, or **paid media**, including paid search and advertising

The distinctions among these three types of media increasingly blur. Some well-resourced communicators create wraparound or omni-channel campaigns that follow their audience as they move from their computer to their phone and beyond. Smaller or less resourced communications teams succeed by focusing on a limited number of channels and executing well—starting with a clear strategy, tracking their data, and refining or pivoting based on results.

Most nonprofits focus the majority of their time and energy on their own channels—including their website, social media profiles, email newsletters, and print communications. Those with greater resources and capacity also invest in earned and/or paid media to drive additional interest and action.

Consistency and persistence are the keys to getting your message across. Our brains are wired to tune out random information in today's noisy world, so repetition across all media is an important strategy to build mindshare.

## Owned media

**Owned media**—the channels your organization manages—includes your:

- Email
- Website
- Social media channels
- Printed collateral (annual report, brochures, flyers)
- Wayfinding, signage, and other site-specific communication

These outlets are essential to building mindshare and deepening engagement with people who already know you. Once you have a person's email address, you can send targeted messages and ask them to take actions that advance your mission (sign up, pledge, donate, advocate, volunteer, etc.). With the exception of social media or email acquisitions, owned media predominantly reaches people who are already on your list. Assuming they opted in, they've got a bigger reason to care and take action on your behalf.

A nonprofit's website is typically its most accessible public address and arguably its most important piece of owned media. It's the first place people entering your active pipeline will likely visit, and where they are most likely to return.

Prioritize building a website that is clear, simple, and enticing. Make it easy for visitors to take action, such as signing up for your email newsletter, providing contact information, or making a donation. Keeping the content on your website accurate, current, and search engine friendly requires updating it frequently—perhaps even daily. Your communications team will likely also have to monitor and maintain the site's security and accessibility and tackle bugs—probably with some help from professional developers.

Communications teams also spend a considerable amount of time producing and managing their organization's newsletter, social media, and other content deployed through their own channels. These efforts collectively are the lifeblood of a healthy, active communications program and each of them requires ongoing care and feeding. The most significant cost of leveraging owned media is the time spent producing and managing it.

## Earned media

Before digital, nonprofits established their voices, engaged, and built mindshare primarily through public relations: writing press releases, developing relationships with journalists, and cultivating media coverage that positioned them as experts. Coverage in a major media outlet meant that large numbers of donors, prospects, and other people would see or read about an organization. That would strengthen an organization's mindshare broadly, reinforce perceptions, and inspire audiences to donate, volunteer, or take other actions.

Today, few channels have the same reach they once had, and consumers' attention has fractured. Earned media channels have proliferated in the past decades and extend well beyond coverage in newspapers, magazines, radio, and TV to the myriad ways content is shared digitally.

PR is no longer a one-size-fits-all media strategy for every nonprofit, although it remains valuable for advocacy organizations because it can help shape the public narrative around an issue. For organizations that don't have an advocacy agenda, earned media is often less valuable. It may make board, staff, and volunteers feel proud to see an organization they are connected with get mentioned in the press, but it is less likely to inspire action than it once was.

## Paid media

Paid media (advertising, lists to rent or purchase, paid search, and more) is the earliest and perhaps most traditional form of marketing. For decades, investing in paid channels meant buying ads in print publications, on TV, on billboards, and via other outlets—and never knowing if the people you wanted to reach actually saw them.

Digital media has made advertising much more targeted. Today, organizations with a budget for paid media can reach very specific people and put very specific messages and actions on their phones and other screens. As they click through to your website or other owned media, they move from being unaware toward considering or taking some sort of action on your behalf. Digital advertising strategies are woven into campaigns that grow a nonprofit's active pipeline.

Remember Smokey the Bear? Keep America beautiful? Schoolhouse Rock? The mind is a terrible thing to waste? The more you know? These public service announcements were a memorable part of most Americans' television experiences for decades.

Public service announcements (PSAs) are a form of advertising that media outlets offer for free because they educate the public. Usually focusing on an issue with wide public benefit (health, safety, literacy, etc.), PSAs use advertising spots to raise awareness and inspire better or healthier behavior. Organizations that produce PSAs typically absorb all of the costs of production (shooting a commercial or producing print ads, for instance) and work with a distribution company that places their ad with networks and other media outlets that run it at no or reduced cost.

## Align the message with the medium

A successful content strategy delivers the right kind of messaging to the right audiences where they're most likely to read and engage with it. Some programs grow rapidly with word of mouth while others rely on social media, advertising, or email to recruit. One advocacy group may send quarterly printed reports; another may produce video or audio content to address key issues important to its audience.

When the Center for Constitutional Rights (*www.ccrjustice.org*) launched the podcast *The Activist Files* in 2018, its goal was to deliver thoughtful conversations directly to people who care about constitutional rights. The podcast features stories of people on the frontlines fighting for justice, including activists, lawyers, and artists, and it helped the Center for Constitutional Rights reach a broader audience.

Effective communicators identify the channels their target audiences prefer and match them with their organization's ability to produce content in that medium. It only makes sense to podcast if the people you're trying to reach generally listen to podcasts—and if your team has the capacity to produce them consistently without relying on one person with podcasting expertise, for example.

Digital content plays an important role in building mindshare in a different way as well. When it's published on your website, digital content provides the keywords search engines need to serve up your website as a resource. Browsers like Google regularly scan every site on the web seeking newly updated content; their algorithms are designed to deliver search results that prioritize the newest and most relevant content that matches the web user's search word or phrase. A successful content program hinges on producing and posting at a steady clip so search engines see it as an active resource. It's a labor-intensive process that requires its own rhythm and momentum.

Many organizations today blog, podcast, host YouTube channels, design data visualizations, and share other content on a monthly, weekly, and even daily basis. All of that content can be used and reused in multiple ways across multiple channels, maximizing their value. You might shoot a video interview with a subject matter expert, edit it into bite-size clips that are shared on social media, and post the transcribed interview on your blog, for example.

Expert communicators monitor what content is viewed and shared the most, using those insights to produce future content. They not only create and curate content, but they also design ways to spark engagement once it's consumed.

When people find useful information about topics they're interested in, their awareness of both the issues and the organization championing them grows, and they are moved toward action.

## ESSENTIAL BUILDING BLOCKS:
## TIME AND MONEY

How long will it take to produce the projects a communications team is responsible for? How much should a nonprofit budget for paid media, search engine marketing, freelancers, and other expenses? There are no standard answers or well-established formulas, but there are ways organizations can get smarter about what they're spending.

No matter how small or large an organization, staff time is often the most critical tool because it is always limited. Knowing what each person's time costs the organization helps managers calculate the expense of all projects and measure return on investment.

### Tracking the value of time

Let's consider an organization that is debating whether it should produce its year-end appeal in-house or outsource it to a company that specializes in this type of work. Estimates from agencies for the project range from $15,000 to $50,000. If it hasn't raised enough money historically to justify spending this much, the organization will probably elect to produce the appeal in-house.

The communications director's previous job was in an organization that tracked staff's time using free software. Each project was given a dedicated task, so it was easy to see who was spending time on each project and run reports to calculate the return on investment. So they recommend a three-month trial of time tracking on this project and others.

Over the duration of the project, staff members spent approximately 100 hours collectively planning, meeting, writing, managing printing and fulfillment, and processing gifts received. Calculating the hourly costs of each staff person involved, this adds up to a soft cost of almost $50,000 to the organization. When all of the gifts are processed, the year-end appeal raises $75,000.

There are several reasons this organization's time investment in the year-end appeal could be worth it. The staff may include excellent fundraisers capable of raising as much or more money than the external agency could. It may also be worth it to grow the team's in-house capacity to fundraise; the costs could be viewed as a capacity-building investment in that case. But if the outside firm might have raised significantly more and the staff had other projects that might have added greater value to the organization, perhaps outsourcing might have cost the organization less in the end.

Lawyers, accountants, and other service professionals typically track their time—often down to the minute. Even when they don't bill by the hour, tracking time helps them measure the true cost of the work they do by clarifying exactly how long it actually takes to complete each task or project. Asking your communications team to track their time, if only for a few months as an experiment, provides data to analyze the costs associated with each project more meaningfully. Without this data, the actual costs of all projects your team produces in-house are masked because they are buried in your overhead.

Most people who start tracking their time are surprised to find that they vastly underestimate how long things actually take. When they realize that they are spending 10 hours a week on a project they thought only took an hour or two, they may question if it's a worthwhile investment of time.

When volunteers or pro bono resources are contributed, identify what they might have cost if you paid for them, too. You'll be able to calculate the true cost to your organization of each project so you can make better decisions as staff, pro bono, and other resources change.

## Calculating staff costs

You can calculate a staff person's cost to the organization using a simple formula:

**Staff person's salary + taxes + benefits (insurance, etc.) = total cost to organization.**

Divide that by the total number of hours a person works each year, including paid time off (for a full-time staff person, that's typically 52 weeks multiplied by 40 hours a week, for a total of 2080).

Although this number won't be exact, it will give you a useful ballpark for what each person's time actually costs the organization per hour.

Using this formula, an employee whose salary is $65,000 might cost the organization roughly $65 per hour. If this person takes 20 hours each month to write and produce the organization's email newsletter, that's a ballpark cost to the organization of $1,300 per issue. Identifying the cost of staff time can help determine if projects should be delegated, outsourced, or managed in other ways to maximize their value.

Looking at staff time as a tangible expense brings an organization's communications budget into sharper focus, helping you make better decisions about which projects to prioritize, what capacities to develop in-house, and how to spend your budget more strategically.

## Budgeting

The 2019 Nonprofit Communications Trends Report (*www.nonprofitmarketingguide.com*) revealed that nearly half of nonprofits (45%) do not have a set communications budget. Eighteen percent report that they spend little to no money beyond salaries, while 27% say they don't have a set budget but find money for expenses as needed. The adaptive ways communications teams work, often dictated by other departments, makes it challenging to standardize budgets across the sector. Communications expenses (such as printing and fulfillment) may also be budgeted to other departments.

In 2015, I facilitated a roundtable discussion about marketing and communications for a dozen or so botanic gardens and parks organizations. Each participant in this group shared their marketing department's size, structure, and budget. Despite many common goals and challenges, there was absolutely no consistency across the group. Some smaller organizations (measured in staff size and annual operating budget) had greater communications resources than their larger peers. They also had widely varied budgets for marketing and communications expenses—ranging from nothing but staff time to as much as 8% of the organization's operating budget.

Despite this variability, there are some logical guidelines that can help any organization budget for communications annually or when planning a special campaign or project. Budget annually for:

- Staff, freelancers, and other consultants your communications team relies on consistently

- Professional development

- Software subscriptions and licenses

- Hardware expenses such as computers and printers (repairs and purchases)

- Ongoing maintenance and upgrades to your website, software, and other assets

- Paid media

What overall percentage of the organization's budget does this amount to? Is that amount logical given the mission and centrality of marketing and communications to the work? An organization whose mission hinges on reaching a specific group (homeless teens, for example) and getting them to take a particular action (entering a program that provides housing and support and helps them stay in school) may need to invest more as a percentage of their overall budget than an organization whose mission is less marketing-dependent (such as a local grant-making community foundation).

Other communications expenses will be periodic or episodic. They may be tied to something finite such as the launch of a new program or campaign or to crisis management, or they could be an investment in the organization's overall communications such as rebranding, a new website, or a new technology. If possible, budget for these occasional costs, including a line item for experiments, separately so they can be adjusted annually.

Whether you're budgeting for the year or for a particular campaign or initiative, consider, at least in the beginning, distinguishing between the musts and the maybes. **Musts** are the essentials: all of the resources you'll need to reach a satisfactory baseline—something that is good enough. **Maybes** are the assets and team expenses that give you a better shot at success reaching and engaging the right people.

Some communicators prefer to plan first and then budget to implement an approved plan. This is an opportunity to explore the possibilities for expanded visibility, reach, and impact, a chance to demonstrate their vision and creativity, and a useful exercise imagining "what if." Leadership would often rather start with a realistic budget and build a communications plan around it so it's fully grounded in reality. But a budget-driven communications plan can miss unique opportunities to leverage new tools, technologies, and relationships, upgrade tired assets, or reinvigorate evergreen campaigns.

Communications staff and leadership who collaborate on the musts and the maybes, exploring what is optimal and pragmatic together—ensuring that the status quo is appropriately reviewed and challenged, and treating the budget and planning process as iterative and collaborative—balance creative new ideas with budget realities. They deepen their shared understanding of what will be most essential from a fiscal and outcomes point of view.

There is practically no limit to how much an organization *could* spend on marketing and communications because paid media and consultant expenses can always expand. If funding existed, just about every organization could invest in growing its engagement by boosting top-of-mind awareness through owned, earned, and paid media. But how much is *enough* to spend? This is the key question every organization explores independently.

## SOFTWARE

Effective communicators measure results, manage projects and media, and more. Without the right software, their efforts will be hampered by lack of data, lack of ability to easily communicate externally, and challenges creating accountability and collaborating with other teams. The following are the basics.

### Project management software

Your communications team will need project management software to track the details, status, and accountable roles on all projects. Ideally, these systems are used interdepartmentally to keep roles and responsibilities clear when collaborating with peers.

Larger organizations encourage or even require all departments to use the same project management system (such as Smartsheet) so everyone can keep track of progress. In smaller organizations, free or low-cost software tools (like Asana, Basecamp, or Airtable) are often used.

Many communicators also use instant messaging programs (like Slack) to stay in touch with their colleagues and collaborators. These programs dramatically reduce email and allow real-time file sharing, video chats, and other exchanges.

## Constituent relationship management

A centralized system that's easy to use and well-maintained is essential to tracking engagement—even more so as you attempt to communicate with people in more nuanced ways (for instance, segmenting based on people's preferences, past engagement, or other variables). Although some organizations still make lists in spreadsheets (gasp!), most now use constituent relationship management (CRM) software to track and manage the details of the people they are connecting with.

These databases can be department-specific, such as Raiser's Edge or DonorPerfect, which are CRM systems designed for and used largely by fundraisers, or they can be more universal, such as Salesforce or Microsoft's Dynamic, which can be customized more broadly so they share information across multiple departments.

## Content management

In the 1990s, websites were built from scratch by developers, often using customized or proprietary code that made it hard for anyone else to change the site. Today's content management systems (CMSs) make it possible for just about anyone with a password to keep your website up to date.

Because maintaining a website no longer requires the ability to code, responsibility for the website has, in most organizations, migrated out of the IT department into marketing or communications. Most CMSs today provide levels of access so multiple members of your staff can contribute, perhaps with different administrative access. WordPress, Drupal, Craft, Squarespace, and others are widely used by nonprofits today. They allow your staff to log in to your website from anywhere, post new content, edit existing pages, and more. They also reduce dependence on one external partner or vendor.

## Email service providers

Email is perhaps the most common tactic that nonprofits use to grow engagement, reinforce a consistent voice, and maintain mindshare. It's also more regulated than you may know.

In 2004, the CAN-SPAM Act of 2003 became law in the United States, requiring businesses that send emails for professional purposes to follow a set of defined practices or risk significant fines. Many other countries have their own regulations about how bulk email and the data that is collected when people engage must be managed, too.

An email service provider (ESP) allows an organization or business to send legally compliant bulk messages. A good ESP helps your organization adhere to legal standards, ensures you follow best practices for elements such as subject lines, and more.

Increasingly, email service providers offer marketing automation services too, allowing communicators to design a set of messages that are triggered by the recipient's behavior. Nonprofits can automatically send specific messages to people who respond to different marketing touchpoints. Watched the video? That triggers an email from the board chair with a request for a donation. Didn't open the email at all? That triggers a "nudge" message to be sent a few days later.

Email service providers range from inexpensive providers (Mailchimp, Vertical Response, and Emma) to enterprise options (HubSpot, Market, Pardot, etc.) that can integrate and sync seamlessly with the data in your CMS. Most ESPs provide your staff with open, click-through, and opt-out rates, along with other data that will be essential to understanding how people are engaging with your organization digitally and comparing your metrics to industry standards.

## Integration

Communicators use data in layered and different ways—for example, overlaying engagement metrics (when someone last visited your website, attended an event, etc.) with donor metrics (recency, frequency, and dollar amount of giving). Integrating your CRM, email provider, and CMS will help ensure that when someone visits your website, opts out, makes a gift, or signs up, your organization has tracked their behavior in a way that allows you to send them personalized messages and provide a seamless experience while adhering to applicable privacy regulations and standards.

Different departments may want to track, use, and control their own data independently. While it can be simpler for your entire organization to use one centralized CRM system, it's not always realistic. In those cases, your team may need software or technical specialists who help each system connect and exchange data where needed, forming a more comprehensive integrated system. Organizations such as Idealware (*www.idealware.org*) and NTEN (*www.nten.org*) can provide tech resources and may help you find consultants with expertise integrating your systems.

# CHAPTER 6

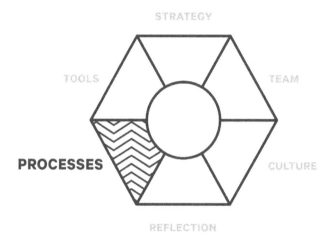

STRATEGY

TOOLS

TEAM

**PROCESSES**

CULTURE

REFLECTION

"It's not the load that breaks you down,
it's the way you carry it."

~ Lena Horne

## WHY PROCESSES MATTER

Clear processes minimize guesswork, reduce barriers that can slow or derail a project, and improve outcomes over time. They also reduce an organization's reliance on individuals and their institutional memory by outlining how things get done so others can implement, too.

Many of the tactics and projects your communications team is responsible for (sending out e-news, crafting appeals, updating web pages, etc.) require following the same steps over and over again to achieve a successful outcome. When people capture these steps in writing they build institutional capacity and sustainable momentum by reducing reliance on any one person's insider expertise.

## CREATING STANDARDIZED WORKFLOWS

Workflows capture the steps necessary to complete a specific task or project—the right way, time after time. If a member of the team leaves, a new person can be trained using the workflow as a step-by-step guide. This reduces reliance on specific individuals and makes it easier for new people to execute potentially complex projects more easily.

In *The Checklist Manifesto: How to Get Things Right*, author Atul Gawande argues that some jobs are now so complicated (think surgeon, engineer, pilot) that it's necessary to have a checklist to reduce human error and ensure that it all goes right. The checklist, a written workflow that everyone can reference, must be so simple to reference and use that it becomes standard operating procedure for the entire team. Gawande's book is full of examples of professional fields where adopting checklists required big shifts in culture. Imagine, for example, nurses reminding doctors to wash their hands properly (as per the checklist) before performing a procedure.

To create sustainable momentum, effective communications teams develop and maintain written procedures and checklists they use consistently and repeatedly. Workflows remove guesswork, reduce human error, and make it easier to onboard new hires. They codify and share implicit knowledge and help ensure critical steps aren't forgotten.

We call this "processifying"—the act of mapping out, in writing, the steps necessary to successfully complete a project. Projects that involve many people and have multiple steps that impact the possible outcome benefit from processification.

Developing and using workflows requires regular moments of reflection to capture and codify essential steps so a project can be re-created efficiently and effectively in the future. Larger marketing or communications departments often have a traffic manager, project coordinator, or project manager, hired for their systems thinking and detail orientation, who's responsible for creating and adjusting the step-by-step process in writing.

Lauren Hall, the chief development officer at the National Brain Tumor Society (*www.braintumor.org*), created the following workflow to ensure her team and colleagues don't miss a beat as they're processing and acknowledging gifts from major donors.

## Gift Agreement Checklist for Major Gifts

*To be completed prior to using the Gift Agreement Template*

1. A donor indicates interest in making a potential major gift.
2. Has this potential gift been vetted and approved as a philanthropic priority?
   2a. If yes, proceed to step 3.
   2b. If no, determine who will need to review and approve this potential gift before moving forward with the donor. In the meantime, thank the donor and provide

a concrete plan for next steps. (*Example: Thank you for your generous consideration of support. With your approval, I would love to share our conversation with [insert appropriate person] at this time, and will be back in touch shortly to discuss next steps with you.*)

3.  Once the potential major gift has been approved, connect with the donor (or the donor's preferred designee) to confirm the following key components of the gift agreement:

    *   Gift amount: $
    *   Endowed fund or current use?
    *   Pledge or one-time payment?
    *   If pledged, define a payment schedule:
    *   Is this gift anonymous?
    *   If not, how does the donor want to be recognized in print?
    *   May the gift amount be recognized publicly?
    *   May the gift priority be recognized publicly?
    *   Are there additional family members who should be recognized publicly?
    *   If so, who is responsible for contacting them about this?
    *   Is a named fund being created by this gift?
    *   If so, what is the proposed name of the fund?
    *   Is named space being created by this gift?
    *   If so, who needs to approve the named space?
    *   What will the named space include (signage, etc.)?
    *   What stewardship actions will be associated with this gift?
    *   Who will spend/oversee the gift at the organization?

- What is the plan if this person leaves the organization?
4. Once all questions have been answered, draft a gift agreement using the Gift Agreement Template.
5. Before sharing the draft gift agreement with the donor, circulate the document for review and approval internally.
6. Once all approvals have been secured, share the draft gift agreement with the donor for review and approval.
   6a. If the donor approves the draft, finalize the document and send it to the donor for their signature. Once it is returned to you, obtain the necessary organizational signatures to fully execute the document.
   6b. Should the donor request any edits to the draft, return to Step 4 and begin again. Please note that any changes to the approved draft may require another round of reviews/approvals before sharing a revision with the donor.
7. Share copies of the fully executed gift agreement with your team, as appropriate. Attach a copy in your donor database, and ensure that all actions related to this gift have been captured.
8. Notify any programs staff or board members associated with the gift, and provide guidance for thanking the donor at this time. If appropriate, schedule a calendar reminder for 6 months to check in with programs staff on any progress updates that may be shared with the donor.
9. Move to the stewardship planning phase.

Workflows capture just enough detail and can also include timelines. The workflow to prepare for a smooth board meeting might look like this:

---

1. Set agenda for the meeting with the executive committee. Send them Board Meeting Template to jump-start the process. (*Start 45 days in advance. Complete one month in advance of meeting.*)

2. Work with staff to prepare all supporting documents and presentations. Remind them to use Board Packet Templates. (*Start one month in advance. Finalize 14 days in advance of meeting.*)

3. Conduct calls to board members requiring clarification or expectation-setting to ensure productive conversations or socialize important new concepts (*Start 14 days in advance. Complete 3 days in advance of meeting.*)

4. Review agenda, documents, and the meeting's run-of-show with staff and board members presenting to confirm/adjust timing and details (*3-5 days in advance*)

5. Confirm tech requirements and logistics of board meeting space (*7 days in advance*)

6. Email board advance reading materials and logistics details (*at least 7 days in advance*)

7. Prepare all hard copies for meeting, walk through facility if new to confirm tech (*day before*)

8.  Arrive early to set up the room, check temperature, put
    up wayfinding signage, and set up tech (*2 hours*)

---

After the meeting, the person who was responsible for
this workflow would immediately add to or adjust it based on
lessons learned to ensure the next meeting went well and set
a reminder to begin the workflow again for the next board
meeting on the schedule.

The steps it takes to create a project or manage a recurring
event may feel so obvious that people are reluctant to write
them down, especially when there's a competent person who's
consistently getting the job done without a checklist. But
what if the terrific staff person who has managed the board
meeting for years departs? What if a step is forgotten that
significantly impacts the outcome? The minimal investment
of time necessary to capture a workflow pays dividends.

Y-USA's (*www.ymca.net*) marketing and communications
team began detailing its systems years ago using spreadsheets,
then using dedicated project management software, and more
recently embraced software that's used to manage projects
organization-wide. Projects requiring support at Y-USA are
triaged and categorized into Tier 1, Tier 2, and Tier 3, each
with anticipated prioritization, budgets, and timelines that
help the team allocate resources thoughtfully from the start.
The level of detail required by the creative team at Y-USA is
deeper than anyone else in the organization collaborating
with them needs, so these documents are typically managed

by their department staff, which includes a dedicated traffic coordinator.

Wendy Currie, the senior creative director in Y-USA's marketing and communications department, led the creation of a process guide to help the team manage projects consistently. Her detailed documentation includes sample project briefs, approval forms, and detailed instructions for the critical phases and steps standard projects move through. It is estimated that the team has experienced a 50% improvement in overall efficiency during each of the first three years it started processifying and executing repetitive projects such as newsletters and magazines according to established workflows.

A note of caution: Creating defined workflows and systems creates challenges and tensions when they are used as weapons to rigidly control projects in ways that can be destructive culturally or create interpersonal friction. Currie and others who use defined workflows are quick to point out that they are guidelines—not hard-and-fast rules—that require adaptation when working with certain peers or in particular contexts.

The best champion for workflows may be a director- or manager-level staff person with a clear aptitude for systems thinking. They should assess which workflows exist and which are missing, starting with the projects your team regularly spends the most time on.

Communications workflows ground a department in consistency and increase the odds that projects will turn out as planned. With that said, the most effective communicators also recognize when circumstances call for something different or unusual and use those opportunities to experiment, off-road, and learn.

Setting individual performance goals around the creation, updating, or use of workflows can motivate everyone to take them seriously. Processifying is, like many things, a muscle that is strengthened through consistent use. Celebrating wins like improved efficiency, reduced human error and downtime during staff transitions or absences, and faster project completion times can help reinforce the value of workflows over time.

## TWO WAYS TO MANAGE PROJECTS

There are many ways communicators can manage projects. The two most common methods are **waterfall** project management and **iterative** project management.

**Waterfall** project management is linear and assumes the project has a beginning, middle, and end: First we plan a project, then we execute it, then we measure its outcomes. Much of the work is done behind the curtain—with the client (who is likely someone in another department) reviewing the work and collaborating at predefined milestones.

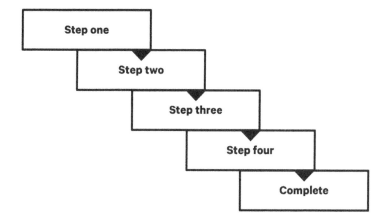

Waterfall project management is useful for projects such as:

- Producing annual reports or brochures
- Rebranding the organization
- Building a new website
- Launching a new campaign
- Any project with a clear end

Other projects have a linear start and finish trajectory only when they are totally overhauled. The rest of the time they benefit from a constant stream of updates and regular work. For projects like these, an **iterative** approach can be beneficial.

**Iterations** are defined periods of time (typically measured in weeks) during which features are developed with heavy collaboration between the people doing the work and the client. This project management approach is newer to nonprofits and most commonly seen in software and other digital companies with a product or service that benefits from constant improvement.

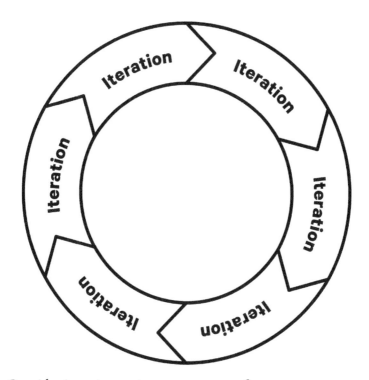

Consider iterative project management for:

- Maintaining the website
- Ongoing social media communication
- Marketing automation "drips" and other evergreen emails
- Any project or deliverable that must keep evolving

Effective communicators iterate to optimize their website, email, social media, and other ongoing projects so they can reduce staff time spent on them, extend the products' shelf life, and improve results. Iterating includes meeting at regular intervals with internal clients to map out the work that will be done in the next iteration, review data and other metrics that reveal outcomes, and assess progress.

# CHAPTER 7

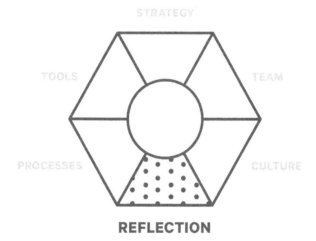

STRATEGY

TOOLS

TEAM

PROCESSES

CULTURE

**REFLECTION**

"If everything was perfect,
you would never learn
and you would never grow."

— Beyoncé Knowles

## WHY REFLECTION MATTERS

Thoughtful reflection—taking the time and space to learn—makes us smarter and more efficient. It's a chance to step out of the details and look around, ask ourselves if it's time to adjust course, stop activities that no longer yield results, and make improvements. For nonprofit communicators and others who manage fast-moving work, a discipline of consistently both looking ahead and looking back helps ensure we stay on track.

## GETTING PERSPECTIVE

What do the 30,000-foot, 20,000-foot, and 10,000-foot views of any communications project or initiative look like at your organization? Is it clear where these projects or initiatives are heading? Do they align with the organization's strategic or annual plans? Do patterns, milestones, and benchmarks emerge? What must be reviewed on a weekly, monthly, quarterly, or annual basis to ensure they stay on course? Bigger-picture questions like these help communicators stay focused and course-correct faster.

Planning lays the foundation for effective reflection because it articulates goals and desired outcomes. Communications plans can support the organization's largest goals (typically articulated in its strategic plan), departmental objectives, or specific projects. Many organizations combine something in writing (a brief, spreadsheet, dashboard, or other tool) with something interpersonal (regular review meetings, debriefs, and other conversations) to reflect on the implementation of and progress against plans.

Nonprofit thought leader Beth Kanter (*www.bethkanter.org*) suggests asking the following questions to spark a moment of reflection:

- What worked well?

- What did we do really well that we don't want to forget the next time we do this?

- What could be improved?

- What could we change?

- What didn't we do that might have worked better?

- What did we learn?

- What surprised us?

- What still puzzles us?

- What questions are not yet answered?

Questions like these remind a team to revisit its strategy and plans, capture and integrate lessons into its systems for future work, and course-correct if needed. They can also be useful in contexts where there is no plan.

## Using research to inform communications strategies

Research helps nonprofit communicators uncover new strategies to achieve their organization's goals and objectives and illuminate key variables that might otherwise have been overlooked. As social media scientist and marketing expert Dan Zarrella says, "Marketing without data is like driving with your eyes closed."

Consumer companies use all types of data to shape every major business function, from product development to advertising to customer service. For nonprofits, insights about their audiences can help them create needed programs and communicate more effectively. Let's look at a couple of hypothetical examples.

MJ's organization was thinking about developing an app designed to engage teenagers in its programs, and the programs staff brought in the communications department to collaborate on the planning. Since teens are always on their phones, the programs staff thought it would be easier to reach and engage them using that channel. When MJ conducted a series of interviews with local teens, obstacles to that assumption they hadn't considered surfaced. Many teens had limited data or pay-as-you-go data plans, so they were disinclined to use any apps they saw as extraneous. Other teens needed their guardians to approve any new apps before they could be installed on their phones, a tiresome process the teens avoided. Other students noted that they were most likely to use the app on school field trips, but that their schools had a "no phones" policy during academic hours. As exciting as the app idea was to the organization, its target audience seemed unlikely to use the app in the ways imagined. Instead, printing booklets and distributing them on-site emerged as a much more likely way to ensure teens got the information the nonprofit wanted them to have.

A large, national organization hired a market research firm to help define its potential for membership growth. The research firm analyzed the profile of existing members and identified how many other Americans fit the same profile, clarifying the potential market for new members. Informed by specific numbers, the organization set numeric targets to grow membership year-over-year that were grounded in reality, not guesswork.

Effective nonprofit communicators use research to learn about the people they are trying to engage. Who are they? What inspires them to act? How do they behave? How can we reach them most effectively? Why should they care? While some organizations budget annually to conduct market research, others do so chiefly around strategic planning or other inflection points.

In 2017, Brooklyn Arts Council (*www.brooklynartscouncil.org*) undertook a strategic planning process. In-depth interviews conducted by an outside strategic planning firm and informal roundtable conversations surfaced new ideas and themes from Brooklyn-based artists, peer organizations, and other key stakeholders.

Because Brooklyn had changed dramatically, as had the external political climate, Brooklyn Arts Council began to rethink who its primary audiences would likely be in the future. But first it needed a clearer picture of its current audience. Who was already engaged with the organization? Grant-seeking artists? Community residents with an interest in the arts? People who work in partner organizations? Analyzing its list of e-news subscribers revealed how they compared to Brooklyn's overall demographics and surfaced useful insights for how the Council might communicate with them in the future.

"We all tell ourselves stories about who our audiences are," says Mark Graham, the director of communications at the American Friends Service Committee (*www.afsc.org*). "Communications can validate and test those stories."

## Types of research nonprofit communicators typically use

*Just Enough Research* by Erika Hall (2013, A Book Apart) is a straightforward, easy-to-read guide to research written for communicators. Hall articulates the types of research communicators typically conduct:

- **Generative or exploratory research**, which helps you identify ideas and insights, such as field observation, literature review, or interviews

- **Descriptive and explanatory research**, which helps you understand how people behave, often in qualitative ways

- **Evaluative research**, which helps you test what's working and what's not, such as usability testing or benchmarking

- **Causal research**, which helps you theorize why something is happening, such as looking at your website's analytics to explore where visitors are coming from

Research can yield powerful results. Dan Stoker, director of analytics for Barack Obama's 2008 presidential campaign, tested different images, videos, and buttons on the splash page of the campaign's website to identify what inspired most website visitors to act. While campaign staff favored one video, test results showed that website visitors didn't; they responded better to still images than videos. On the Optimizely.com blog, Stoker wrote that the winning variation of image and button had a sign-up rate of 11.6% versus 8.26% on the original page, an improvement of 40.6%. He estimates this test helped the campaign acquire two million new email addresses, resulting in 288,000 more volunteers and an additional $60 million in donations.

Testing, a powerful form of evaluative research communicators use, can improve results by helping you incrementally tweak the elements that inspire people to respond and engage. Will more people complete your donation landing page when there is a photograph at the top or if there are no photos? Will their average gift size change as a result? Do more people open your e-news when the subject line of the email features topic A or B?

Federal records in the early 2000s indicated that children diagnosed with Duchenne muscular dystrophy (DMD) seemed to be dying younger in particular states. With funding earmarked to investigate and launch initiatives to reduce mortality, Parent Project Muscular Dystrophy (*www.parentprojectmd.org*), identified Mississippi as the optimal place to pilot this program. On-the-ground research identified how children in Mississippi with DMD were identified, diagnosed, and cared for; what programs and other resources were available; and how parents navigated the diagnostic and care journey. Research also revealed doctors with limited or no experience diagnosing DMD and significant challenges patients experienced accessing medical care in low-income rural communities. It appeared that children were either misdiagnosed or not diagnosed at all, so they were less likely to receive life-extending treatments.

Parent Project Muscular Dystrophy launched a multipronged campaign to increase the odds that kids with DMD would be identified and diagnosed earlier. It included training for preschool teachers and Head Start program facilitators, educational resources for rural healthcare system medical professionals, and an outreach campaign featuring a public service announcement and other ads. During the campaign's pilot period, nine children with Duchenne muscular dystrophy were identified and diagnosed, a significantly higher number than was expected given the rarity of this disorder. Intake tracking (another form of evaluative research) showed that all of their families had seen the public service announcement on television and reached out for more information.

Piloting the program and its outreach efforts in Mississippi helped Parent Project Muscular Dystrophy test a number of ways to reach its target audience and engage them to take action, leading to earlier diagnosis. As the program expanded, the lessons learned during the pilot about how to build mindshare for Duchenne were put into practice.

Effective research begins by challenging your assumptions. How is your organization seen and understood by the people you need to engage to advance your mission? How will they interact with you? What realities impact what they want or need from you? These assumptions are often stated (explicitly or implicitly) in the plans and project briefs communicators develop at the start of a new project, and can be an excellent basis for conducting research.

At the start of any significant new initiative or at key junctures along the way, pressure-test your team's assumptions (which may be rooted in implicit or explicit bias or misinformation) with research. Use it to confirm or debunk your team's assumptions, define the intangible, and illuminate the best path forward.

# TURNING DATA INTO INSIGHT

Crisis Text Line (*www.crisistextline.org*) provides free support to people in crisis via text messaging. The staff includes data scientists who help the organization use the information it collects from its users to improve the quality of support it provides. By analyzing data from previous texters, the technology team has built a tool that identifies users who are at the greatest risk of suicide and pushes their texts to the front of the queue, ensuring they are responded to fastest. Data reflection is a powerful component of the organization's work; it reports trends, publishes research, and invites collaboration with other individuals and groups responding to those in crisis. Crisis Text Line exemplifies how deeper data analysis, insights, and integration can create better client experiences and help the entire organization—not just its communications team—improve.

Data science, the discipline of analyzing data sets to answer questions and reveal insights, is a relatively new field that is increasingly making its way into the nonprofit sector.

The Union of Concerned Scientists (*www.ucsusa.org*) has a communications team of 27 people, including content and engagement specialists. When Suzanne Shaw, the Union's director of communications, sought to expand the engagement team, she hired a data analyst who reports to the director of engagement. Having in-house data analysis allows the communications team to regularly review and report the results of their work. In an organization that includes many scientists, this analysis increases the communications team's credibility with peers in other departments.

Not all organizations need data scientists or people with advanced technical skills who can build complex algorithms on staff, however. Communications staff and their peers in programs, development, and other departments can collaborate to ask key questions, make sure that the data they capture and use is stored and maintained effectively, and create moments of reflection that yield insights. They might also collaborate with internal or external evaluators.

Your organization's programs, development, and other data can be used to:

- **Compare your organization's results to peers':** Are your outcomes comparable to, greater than, or less than those of other organizations? Are you crushing it or falling short of the industry?

- **Measure results:** Did you achieve what you set out to do? Is the work moving the needle?

Enlisting communicators to assist with data analysis can help your organization gather insights from a specific department's work and leverage them organization-wide. Effective communicators can translate these lessons into audience profiles and mindsets, craft brand assets that are more compelling, and share lessons learned with other departments.

## Aggregating data into scorecards and dashboards

Each department in a nonprofit has its own key performance indicators (KPIs) and metrics. Fundraisers track retention rates, lifetime value, and other data that illuminates donors' behavior, commitment, and engagement. Programs staff track how many people apply, accept, attend, and return. Communications, whose success is dependent on other departments achieving their goals, is uniquely positioned to share insights organization-wide and to report on overall engagement with the mission. Communications may also track external awareness of the organization and its mission more generally, measuring how well-known and understood the brand is.

Dashboards and scorecards provide perspective for moments of constructive reflection by revealing patterns and shifts in KPIs over time. By reviewing measurable data about how people are engaging on a weekly or monthly basis, your team can identify what's working well and where improvements could be made, and spot trends when things change.

CFLeads (*www.cfleads.org*) helps community foundations build strong communities by advancing effective practices, sharing knowledge, and galvanizing action on critical issues of our time. They track engagement with their mission in a multilayered dashboard built in an Excel spreadsheet using data from event RSVPs and attendance, new and returning funders, and content performance. It's a simple, low-tech tool that's fast and easy to maintain.

The communications team at the American Friends

Service Committee (*www.afsc.org*) developed a digital dashboard that pulls data from varied sources throughout the organization and expresses engagement visually. Quantifying how people build mindshare and take action on behalf of AFSC helps them identify strengths and opportunities for growth organization-wide.

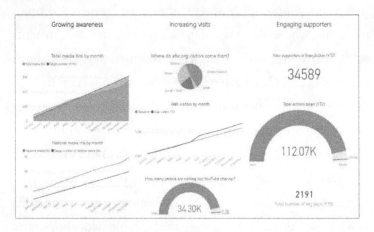

*AFSC's 2018 dashboard, first iteration*

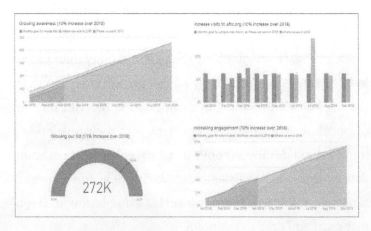

*AFSC's updated dashboard for 2019*

American Friends Service Committee's communications
and programs teams hold quarterly meetings to review their
KPIs, reflect together, and make new plans or adjust their
communications for the upcoming quarter.

Nonprofit communications dashboards rely on data from
owned media (website, social media, and email activity in
particular) and fundraising and programs CRM systems. An
abundance of free dashboard templates from Google, CRM
systems, and other software companies can jump-start the
process of setting up dashboards.

Management guru Peter Drucker noted that what gets
measured gets managed. Effective communicators define
their organization's most important engagement indicators
collaboratively with each department, then track and report
on them regularly. Creating a discipline of weekly, monthly,
quarterly, and annual measuring and reporting within your
communications team will help ensure that everyone is clear
about how effectively their work is reaching and engaging the
people who will advance the mission.

# CHAPTER 8:
# BUILDING AND OPTIMIZING YOUR ORGANIZATION'S COMMUNICATIONS ENGINE

## FOCUSING ON WHAT COMMUNICATIONS SHOULD ACHIEVE

In Chapter 1, we defined three goals for communications:

- **Engagement:** The right people know, remember, and connect with your organization and its work, then take meaningful action on its behalf.

- **Clear voice:** Your organization's voice is clear, credible, compelling, and consistent at all points of contact.

- **Sustainable momentum:** Your organization's communications are not dependent on an individual.

The six components explored in the previous chapters—Strategy, Team, Culture, Tools, Processes, and Reflection—are the components necessary to achieve these goals. But where should you start?

I suggested earlier you keep a notebook to capture your

vision for successful communications in your organization, your thoughts on what's getting in the way, and the ideas that surfaced for how to optimize it. Those notes plus the score from the self-assessment in Chapter 1 may have already revealed the most important areas where you can start optimizing your nonprofit's communications.

If your nonprofit already successfully builds engagement, has a clear voice, and has some sustainable momentum, start by assessing and optimizing your strategy, teams, culture, tools, processes, and reflection—in that order. You'll find many of these elements are already firmly in place and others can get stronger by implementing some of the ideas in this book.

If not, start by identifying the communications goal that will have the greatest impact once your organization strengthens or achieves it. Will you benefit the most from building engagement? Developing your organization's clear voice? Or creating more sustainable momentum?

## Building engagement

Building engagement will likely consume the most resources and require the greatest effort, regardless of an organization's size, mission, or age. It may also be the most directly effective way communicators can help advance the mission.

Start by clarifying what's working, what's missing, and what should be improved with your current efforts. Do your organization's communications effectively engage the right people to take action? Are the issues you address and the work you do clear to them? Answer those questions by revisiting your answers to the self-assessment in the first chapter and through discussion with your organization's leadership and your communications team. Then summarize your objectives to improve your engagement. That exercise might look like one of these examples:

*While our target audiences are clear about the issues we fight for, they may not see us as the conduit through which they should take action. Our objective is to increase engagement with people who value the issue by doubling our list of activists in the next two years and sparking at least 25% of our list to take one of the following actions: sign a pledge, attend a rally, or attend our legislative advocacy event.*

*We are unclear who our primary audiences really are and how they feel about us. By the end of this year, we will have conducted research necessary to define the top three personas and mindsets we must engage to successfully advance the objectives outlined in our strategic plan, and we will have developed a comprehensive communications plan to engage them that's tied to realistic resources.*

*We successfully inspire people to attend events and take other actions, but rarely do they demonstrate their support by making a donation, too. We will measure what percentage of people who've taken some other action also supported us with a gift in the past few years, compare our results to those of peer organizations, and create a plan to reach a realistic target this fiscal year.*

Each of these statements outlines a challenge and sets an objective. They also form the basis of a brief (Chapter 2: Strategy). Expand on this brief by using or developing the other elements in that chapter (audience personas and mind-sets, an engagement framework, and communications plans). Get feedback on the document you create from members of the different departments it impacts—communications, government relations, development, etc.—to capture your team's expertise and build their buy-in. You've got the start of a communications strategy.

Assess your existing communications team, culture, tools, processes, and reflection using this strategy as a yardstick. Do you have what you need to make it happen? Identify your organization's current strengths, weaknesses, opportunities, and threats (SWOT) by examining each area.

## Clear voice

Crafting a clearer, more consistent voice for your organiza-tion often begins with a branding process to update or create powerful new assets. Rebranding processes are typically (and usually most effectively) led by expert consultants, not by in-house teams. Most organizations review their brand assets every few years (right after strategic planning) but generally don't make large changes unless there's been a significant shift.

The ongoing work of ensuring an organization's voice is clear, credible, compelling, and consistent at all points of contact is powered by your in-house team. The processes they use to integrate brand assets into all the writing, speaking, and designing of external communications largely shape how external audiences will perceive your organization's voice—and therefore help shape your organization's mindshare.

REFLECTION                    *199*

## Sustainable momentum

Many organizations become dependent on individuals who manage and execute communications projects, putting sustainable momentum in jeopardy. Exploring these questions can help you determine if you've built a communications engine that can function independently of key people:

- Do we have documented communications workflows and systems that help our team execute projects effectively? Can new people quickly get up to speed on the work?

- Are the workflows regularly updated, referenced, and maintained?

- Are we dependent on a few people with institutional memory or specialized knowledge to get things done?

- Would we be able to communicate well if key people left the organization unexpectedly— without rebuilding from scratch?

If the answers to these questions reveal a lack of sustainable momentum, start by defining processes that will enable your team to work more efficiently and build capacity. Many people who manage communications teams have no formal project management background. With a little professional development (and perhaps project management certification) they'll see the value of creating tools, workflows, and systems that can be used without relying on any individual.

# KEEPING YOUR COMMUNICATIONS
# ENGINE HUMMING

Building engagement, communicating with a clear voice, and creating sustainable momentum are not one-time achievements. Maintaining a communications engine in good working order capable of consistently meeting these goals requires an ongoing practice and moments of reflection about all six components.

Assess progress regularly to ensure your communications engine continues to run smoothly. Solicit input on communications and how it's achieving the organization's desired outcomes from staff periodically, repeat the self-assessment in Chapter 1 every one to two years, and update your communications strategy and plan as needed. A healthy, collaborative dynamic between the executive director and the person who's responsible for external communications within the organization will be key.

## Progress—not perfection

Every new tool, better process, or sharper strategy that you put in place will help your nonprofit's communications engine grow stronger. Every person who augments your team or positively shapes the culture will too. Incremental progress is the only, and perhaps best, way to do this work. Over time, the results will be clear and profound.

# THANKS

Thank you to all of the people who work in nonprofit organizations that have shared their stories and experiences with me over the past two decades, and who have put these ideas to the test. A particular shout-out to the amazing people who served as beta readers throughout this process.

Thanks to the excellent people at Big Duck who have turned some of my sketchy ideas into game-changing communications tools and processes over the past 25 years. Elizabeth Ricca and Farra Trompeter, in particular, have been essential partners on this journey. Thanks also to the current team at Big Duck, who've helped identify patterns, pressure-test this model, and allowed me the time and space to do this work.

Christine Borgford, Julia Cassell, Bryn Mooth, Daisy Prescott, Rinku Sen, Jaime Sperling, and Meghan Templehof really helped this book come together and made it stronger.

Above all, my thanks to Craig, Kate, Abi, and Mindy, who make anything seem possible because they give me so much love, support, and joy. And because they feed me.

# SARAH DURHAM

Sarah is an entrepreneur and creative consultant with a passion for helping nonprofits communicate more effectively so they can advance their missions.

She founded Big Duck (*www.bigduck.com*) in 1994 to help nonprofits increase their visibility, raise money, and communicate more effectively. In 2019, she acquired Advomatic (*www.advomatic.com*), which builds and supports websites for nonprofits. She spends her days guiding these businesses and talking with nonprofit leaders about their communications.

The author of *Brandraising: How Nonprofits Raise Visibility and Money Through Smart Communications* (Jossey-Bass/ Wiley, 2010), Sarah's expertise has been borrowed by NPR, *The Chronicle of Philanthropy*, Guidestar, and others. She is a sought-after speaker on branding, fundraising, and other nonprofit communications topics. She was named a "top fundraiser under 40" by *Fundraising Success* magazine in 2006, and one of the most influential women in technology by *Fast Company* magazine in 2010. As an adjunct professor at NYU's Robert F. Wagner Graduate School of Public Service, Sarah taught strategic communications to other aspiring nonprofit communicators for many years.

Sarah is a native New Yorker who lives in Brooklyn with her extremely handsome husband, Craig, and exceptionally brilliant daughters, Abigail and Kate.

CPSIA information can be obtained
at www.ICGtesting.com
Printed in the USA
LVHW051250230520
656337LV00011B/432/J